"When it comes to talking about faith, Antoinette Bosco is one of the most believable authors you will ever read. She knows, deep in her heart and right down to her toes, what she is talking about, and she talks about it in ways that will keep you turning the pages long after your bedtime. She knows that faith depends on God, not us. So read this book and prepare to find your faith much more alive than it was before. Thank you, Toni, for such a good, good book."

Mitch Finley
Author, *101 Ways to Nourish Your Soul*

"*Shaken Faith* is an honest and courageous book by someone brave enough to admit what each of us knows: even the strongest believer will experience times when God seems far away. By sharing her pain, her darkness, her joys and the insights of her own faith-struggle, Antoinette Bosco has given readers the gift of knowing that it's O.K. to doubt, because we have the assurance that God's love for us is steadfast even when our faith in him is not."

Peggy Eastman
Author, *Godly Glimpses: Discoveries of the Love That Heals*
Editor, *Share* magazine

"Like winter trees which have lost their leaves, *Shaken Faith* clears our vision, revealing the source of hope and strength in our lives. Antoinette Bosco shows that even when our faith is shaken by tragedy or loss, the experience may actually propel us toward a more deeply rooted trust in God. These stories of faith share her life journey with God who sustains and inspires her work for justice, a fruit of her shaken and rooted faith."

Rosemarie Greco, DW
Director, Wisdom House Retreat Center, Litchfield, CT

"*Shaken Faith* is written from and for the heart. Writing from the depths of her own faith-shaking moments, Antoinette Bosco shows the path to faith: faith in ourselves, faith in life, and faith in the God whose arms surround us at every moment. Your heart will be touched and come alive again as you read this remarkable book."

Father Paul Keenan
Author, *Stages of the Soul* and *Heartstorming*

Shaken
Faith

Hanging in There
When God Seems Far Away

ANTOINETTE BOSCO

TWENTY-THIRD PUBLICATIONS
A Division of Bayard PO BOX 180 • MYSTIC, CT 06355
1-800-321-0411 • FAX: 1-800-572-0788 • E-MAIL: ttpubs@aol.com

DEDICATION

I dedicate this book to my beautiful sister Rosemary, who has always been there for me since the day I became her "little sister," who gave me the gift of her fidelity, who introduced me to music, who never, ever faltered in her love for me.

The Scripture passages contained herein are from the *New Revised Standard Version of the Bible,* copyright © 1989, by the Division of Christian Education of the National Council of Churches of Christ in the U.S.A. All rights reserved.

Twenty-Third Publications
A Division of Bayard
185 Willow Street
P.O. Box 180
Mystic, CT 06355
(860) 536-2611
(800) 321-0411

ISBN:1-58595-131-5
Library of Congress Catalog Card Number: 00-135773
Printed in the U.S.A.

ACKNOWLEDGMENTS

The seed for this book was planted many years ago after I was invited to write a small booklet on faith by Emilie Cerar, the editor of Resurrection Press and a longtime friend. But it was the experiences of the past five years that actually brought me to the decision to write a book on faith, and for this I must thank Neil Kluepfel, publisher of Twenty-Third Publications.

After he published my book, *The Pummeled Heart: Finding Peace Through Pain*, I began hearing from so many people who, like myself, were hurting from tremendous loss. Because of this, my work changed almost radically, and I went from being primarily a writer to entering into a personal ministry of helping people who called on me, people who often desperately needed to talk to someone who could understand their pain. In most cases, their faith had been shaken. They were on a tightrope, confused about whether they believed in God and goodness, or not. These people needed to hear it was all right to feel angry at God sometimes. They needed to know that if they could trust that God had not abandoned them, they would find a great prize—a transformed faith which would give them a new understanding and vision about the relationship between us and God.

And so I felt it was time for me to write a book which expressed what I have learned from working with so many great people. Neil Kluepfel agreed, and I owe him much thanks for believing in me.

I also am immensely grateful to my children, Sterling, Paul, Mary, Margaret, and Frank, to my daughters-in-law, Bernadette, Judi, and Sue, to my son-in-law Rick, to my grandchildren, sisters, brothers, and friends for all the affirmation they have always given me. They have encouraged me to continue in my hope that I can serve God and the world through my writing.

A few segments in this book appeared in columns I have written since 1975 as a syndicated columnist for the Catholic News Service in Washington, DC, and in the booklet I wrote for Resurrection Press. It has been my privilege to write for both.

C O N T E N T S

Introduction

A few years back, I was asked to give a talk for a Communion breakfast scheduled for Palm Sunday. It struck me that this was a strangely special time to be giving a talk, that is, at the very beginning of Holy Week, a time when we were to walk again with Jesus on his difficult journey toward the cross and his death.

I had always had mixed feelings about the fact that Jesus had to die to save us. As a parent, I struggled with a Father who expected his son to suffer so much. At the risk of sounding disrespectful, it had sometimes seemed to me that God was asking too much. More than that, considering Jesus's final cry of despair, I always wondered if the Father was there to help Jesus during his last earthly moments.

These were some of the thoughts that took over as I began to plan my talk. The title that kept coming out as I pondered was an off-beat one. Still, I decided to go with it: "Is God a Deadbeat Dad—or a Passionate Lover?" I sent this title off to the parish where I was going to give the talk. When the priest announced the talk at Sunday Mass the next week, he heard titters from the congregation. With great good humor, he quickly reacted, saying, "I don't write these. I only announce them." At that, the congregation howled.

Putting that talk together was one of the most soul-searching experiences I had ever had. God a deadbeat Dad? You all know that expression: deadbeat Dads are fathers who abandon their families, who don't support their kids. Well, we've called God "our Father" all our lives—and yet sometimes we have to ask, what kind of a father is he anyway? Look at this world. It is racked with injustice and disease, wars, violence, and hatred. It is filled with people losing jobs, getting cancer, having car accidents, seeing marriages break up, and dealing with kids on drugs.

1

I would wager that everyone reading this has felt abandoned by God at least once in life, and has wondered: where is my father when I need him? These are the times when we worry that maybe we have lost our faith—and hey, maybe for a while, we do. Even the great mystic Teresa of Avila complained that she was maligned, persecuted, and physically suffering—the works! She told God outright, "If this is the way you treat your friends, no wonder you have so few of them."

Boldly, I say that every suffering calls into question the goodness of God and presents a challenge to our faith. But what is faith?

In my younger years, I could polarize faith into something as cut and dried as "certainty" versus "disbelief." When I got older I learned that faith really deals with growth, the human problem of the ever moving and evolving relationship of humankind with something greater than ourselves. And that is the point when my faith got fuzzy and fractured. It became harder to believe; more than ever, I yearned for a strong faith. God would become elusive, like a deadbeat Dad, and I would go searching for him. Indeed, God was there all the time, but I didn't always know this.

I came to accept that God is our mysterious relative: our origins are in this God. But this God exists in an order different from what we know. And we don't like this. We want answers. We think we deserve answers. I once asked my departed son, Peter—I talk to him all the time since he left this earth at the age of twenty-seven— why it is that no one has ever come back to earth after dying to tell us clearly and precisely that life goes on, and to let us know what happens when we enter the next world. Clearly, I received an answer: "That's because you would never be able to understand."

There is so much more to God than we could ever, ever comprehend. Some theologians have used the example of a caterpillar to try to help us understand the mystery of the vastness of God. Could a caterpillar imagine or understand that it will become a butterfly?

Strangely, it has been my pain that has opened up so many insights about God. Before life brought me severe trials, I thought my faith was strong, that it gave me all the answers I needed about life, and that it would always be my comfort. Now I know differently. I have learned that faith is really Mystery. I will never have the answer to why God looks like a deadbeat Dad so often. But guess what? I've learned that it doesn't matter. If we are people of faith, we accept the limitations that come with life because there is so much more to life, so much more that we have other than just answers to our questions.

I have listened to myself and others talk about our trials of faith. Often, the problem is we want God to reorder the cosmos to cater to our needs, and when this doesn't happen we feel our faith is fractured. But if we set up unrealistic expectations for God, we doom our faith from the start, just as we would any relationship. We cannot make God an extension of our desires. When it comes to God, the adage "seeing is believing" goes into reverse. Believing is seeing. Believing is faith.

Having faith does not mean that life will be like walking in a rose garden. Pope John XXIII put it well:

> Above all, one must always be ready for the Lord's surprise moves, for although He treats His loved ones well, He generally likes to test them with all sorts of trials, such as bodily infirmities, bitterness of soul, and sometimes opposition so powerful as to transform and wear out the life of the servant of God, the life of the servant of the servants of God, making it a real martyrdom.

For a Christian, faith converges in Jesus, whose basic and fundamental message is that God loves us with no strings attached. Jesus asked us to have a faith with such outrageous power that it could move mountains. His message is enduring and for all.

I have come to trust that no matter how much I have wavered in doubt or stood in darkness, no matter how loud and fierce my cries of pain became, I was never in real danger. For I trusted that I was always within the arms of the God who loves me.

I have written this book to share that trust.

Faith Is Ever Elusive

Every sort of energy and endurance, of courage and capacity for handling life's evils, is set free in those who have religious faith.
▶ WILLIAM JAMES

For those of us who call ourselves Christians, the question of faith is a crucial one as we start a new millennium. In the midst of a restless world and a changing Church, we are being forced to re-examine the meaning of faith in our lives. Are we facing a crisis of faith with an uncertain, negative outcome? Or is a new understanding of faith emerging—a new promise of partnership between God, people, and the realities of modern life, foreshadowing a new level of growth in Christian faith among the people of God?

Any attempt to define faith will cause difficulties because faith centers on where we stand in relation to God, his created world, and, for Christians, the Church. Questions are continually being raised about the problem of belief and the relevance of faith in our times, and I have found that answers are elusive.

I once brought a group of Catholic women together, and asked what their faith meant to them and how they would define it. Like me, they realized two things: there is a natural faith, a kind of trust that allows one to get up, walk out the door, and not worry that a speeding car will run you down. But more than that, there is a supernatural faith which leads us to believe that a good God has revealed himself to his creatures on earth and that our creator seeks a response from each of us.

The women in the group said things like "Our response to faith is a daily challenge, bound up with everyday living," and "A life without faith is one engulfed in darkness." Yet as we further discussed what faith actually was, it was hard to get to a really precise definition. Some said they saw faith as simply facing the realities of life, both good and bad, while hanging on to God for dear life. Others said faith meant accepting that God is a "mystery God" who sometimes seems very close and sometimes seems very far away. One mother put it this way: "Faith is something you can't reach out and touch, yet it is something you hold on to."

Another woman, who had suffered some severe losses in her recent past, said she no longer called faith a comfort, but a "pain." To her, "faith now means the willingness to be jolted out of your comfortable position. It is the person of faith, for example, who is willing to be jeered at for working for gay rights or prison reform, who is willing to have his or her life disrupted for a principle. This is pain."

One woman called faith the "activator" in her life, describing this as "looking for what God has to say to you":

> You run a house on practically no budget, and yet manage to feed a big family—that's faith. A man works sixteen hours a day at two jobs and comes home every night never giving up—that's faith. A woman has small kids and her husband has a heart attack, yet she manages to keep going and still help others—that's faith. I believe all the happenings of each day, whether they bring you good things or difficult things, have a purpose rooted in what God asks of us. God gives each of us something to do, and faith means we don't turn our back on what he's asking.

Still another woman said, "I personally have always been tantalized by trying to understand how faith operates in the life of a human person. One thing I have come to learn is that God comes to no one as a complete package to be accepted or rejected. He must continually be discovered."

There was wisdom in everything the women said. Yet when we tried to put the precise meaning of faith into words, we stumbled.

I once again grappled with how to talk about faith when I was asked to be a speaker for a lenten series called "Faith Works," being put on by an Episcopal church. It struck me that the title was a double-edged gem. Use the word "works" as a noun, and it becomes our part of the challenge of faith. Use it as a verb, and it describes what God does. And so I prepared my talk starting with the fact that faith is not one-sided: it takes two to have faith.

So often we don't focus enough on this two-way connection because of our limited definitions of faith. I realized this many years ago when a man in a religious discussion group told me he envied me for my faith. He said, "You're so lucky. You have the faith."

"The faith?" I asked. "Is it a thing? Something you hold and look at?"

I think he said what he did because he thought of faith as a gift. Years ago, and still today, Christians did indeed refer to faith as being a gift. And it isn't a bad way of putting it. A gift can't fall out of the sky; it comes to us from a giver. Where there is faith, there is always a giver. For faith is never generated out of a vacuum. Our faith is a share in something—Someone—tremendous, never just an isolated package in itself.

Yet thinking of faith as a gift became a stumbling block for me, for I had learned that faith is not a gift as we ordinarily define it. Faith is not "ours" in the sense that it is constant or consistent, always close, always comforting. Faith is a sometimes win, sometimes lose struggle. When faith is firm, life makes sense. But when it is elusive, we are like non-swimmers who have lost our water wings, and life itself wavers from nonsensical to terrifying.

What the man in the discussion group didn't know about me

was that I was always on a tightrope about my faith. It went like this: "Yes, I believe, no, I don't. Lord, help my unbelief!"

Having struggled with faith, concluding that it was not a gift, I began to see it as a relationship between me and Christ/God. Being a relationship, faith had an energy of its own, sometimes positive, sometimes negative. It then became clear to me that there truly is a gift of faith, and that is baptism. Baptism brings us to the faith community, to the place where Christ's existence comes alive for us. It is the place where the relationship between the Triune God and each one of us begins. I now saw baptism and faith as two sides of the same coin.

My heritage is Italian-American and for my people, the necessity and importance of baptism was as self-evident as the necessity of eating. The birth of every Italian baby was properly celebrated with immediate plans for its "Christian-ing." My grandmother told me many times that in her hometown in southern Italy, birthdays were not important but baptismal days were celebrated each year for this marked the real birth of a person. Godparents were properly named "compadre" and "commadre," meaning co-father and co-mother.

The Italian celebration of baptism helped me understand the complexity of this sacrament. Baptism isn't something that is done once and finished; it goes on and on. Baptism does not end with the initiation of a person into the faith community—in this case, the Church. Baptism is also an immersion, symbolized by the water essential to the sacrament, where a person is plunged into the life of Christ, wears his skin, shares his blood, bears his cross, and dies with him so that Christ's mission will be continued. Being initiated into the community of Christ is the beginning of the process. But it is no guarantee that a person will choose to accept the continual baptism, the immersion, and all the situations to come which demand fidelity to Christ. To remain valid, baptism must be lived—and that is where it becomes linked to faith.

As initiation into Christhood, baptism is the gift. But to give meaning to this initiation one must, as the apostle Paul says, "put on Christ" and become the new person, so that "it is no longer I who live, but it is Christ who lives in me. And the life I now live in the flesh I live by faith in the Son of God, who loved me and gave himself for me" (Gal 2:20). This is faith. The gift and the relationship are inseparable, two sides of the same coin.

What happens from then on is the great unknown, the challenge. If faith is a relationship between Christ/God and me, it is living and growing. Like all relationships, it has its highs and its lows, its missing moments and its times when you are on the verge of a split, facing the end of togetherness and the despairing loneliness that comes with the loss of faith.

A living relationship

The experiences of my life have taught me that faith is a living relationship. I remember a time when I was twenty-five years old. My second baby, John, was then six weeks old, critically ill and near death from pneumonia. My ex-husband was already mostly absent, interested in pursuits other than family. I was angry at God. I felt betrayed and helpless and abandoned. I desperately bargained for my child's life, while screaming for meaning in my own.

That was when I realized faith was not a set of dogmas or a security blanket. I didn't really know then what my faith was. I realized, however, I was wrestling with a relationship because I was crying out to God, "What do you want of me?" You don't scream at or bargain with a gift—only with a person. When I heard myself saying, "Why have you forsaken me?" I caught the ring of familiarity. I knew those words. I wasn't the first person to say them. And that marked the true beginning of my quest to know—really know— Jesus. We had something very much in common: a feeling of abandonment.

I would wager that anyone reading this can empathize with what I am saying. If you have been trying to live a life of faith, that is, if you have been trying to grow in a relationship with the person who gives meaning to your very existence, you have probably experienced high points. These are the exhilarating moments when you soar and think you will never be alone or sad again. And you have probably experienced the low places, where you find yourself isolated, terrified that you have lost touch with the source of your life. These times, when you are in a spiritual desert, are the seasons in hell, lifeless, motionless times.

Faith can break us out of that awful isolation because faith is the only link, the only connection to the source and meaning of our life. Faith is difficult. It is challenging. It is painful. It is joyful. It grows. It erodes. It grows again. It is a relationship.

Paul Wilkes wrote a book about what he learned from meditation in a monastery. He spoke of how faith will teach us, but will "also extract its due. Faith asks that each of our souls be stripped bare...so as to present ourselves before God without trappings or conceits, titles or goods. It asks of us that we present our deepest selves, unprotected by any of the overlays with which the world has camouflaged us." This is what all beautiful and honest relationships require; no wonder they are so complex.

Sometimes what people call "faith" is more honestly a quest for certainty carried out by adhering to formulas: do this and all will be fine. Some people fall into the confusion of substituting devotions for faith: for example, attend Mass on the nine First Fridays and you will certainly get to heaven; put a St. Christopher medal in your car and you will avoid accidents; make a novena and your prayers will be answered; say the family rosary and the family will stay together. Attending First Friday Mass, making novenas, and saying a family rosary are all admirable activities, but they are devotions—an adjunct to faith, but not faith itself. They are scaffolding, helpful on the climb to our destiny. But it is faith which keeps us moving. Faith is a journey, and the challenge of this faith journey is to learn how to identify and avoid the distractions and temptations that would erode our relationship with Christ.

Decades ago, Karl Rahner, an outstanding theologian and scholar, urged his colleagues to undertake the task of "leading men not to the formulas of faith, but to the mystery of God himself," so that Christianity will no longer seem to "consist of such an abundance of declarations, dogmatic and moral tenets and assertions by the Church that we can hardly see the forest for the trees."

That statement was disturbing to some Catholics back then. But the time had come for change. Faith would now need to be seen in more dynamic terms. According to the Rev. Francis M. Tyrrell, a retired professor of theology at Immaculate Conception Seminary on Long Island, faith must be seen as

...a life that is in continuous dialogue with God...as that knowledge which grows out of a love relationship between two persons—God who calls us to be faithful sons and daughters, and we who respond to him. In the past we tended to think of faith as an intellectual assent to doctrines proposed by the Church as revealed by God under the influence of grace. This made it too much of a matter of merely intellectual commitment—which is only one element in the total picture of faith.

God has manifested himself to me through Christ, the Scriptures and the Church—in its preaching of that gospel and in the sacraments, through which he gives himself to me personally under signs. But he also reveals himself to me in the various human relationships and events in my life—in friendships and love as well as tragedies and joys. All these are vehicles of his personal will for me.

God has put us on our own. The relationship is not childlike dependence. Nor can we blame him for every misfortune. God has not given us answers—only the awareness of the context in which we are facing these problems. Christian faith is not an easy answer to life's hard times, but it is a strengthener and a fortifier, a light and motivation with which to face life's problems.

For if Christ could face death and make of it redeeming significance, it is possible, through difficulties, for us to realize that no tragedy is without some meaning, even though we may never know what this is.

One of the truths that makes faith so difficult is that we don't have answers to many of our deepest questions. This is especially so when we have suffered loss and are plagued with asking "why?"

and get only silence in return. That is when faith becomes really elusive and you learn it was never meant to be defined, only accepted with fidelity—as is the case with any relationship. You end up saying, as I continually do, faith means accepting mystery.

In a book written long ago, Eugenia Price asked, "Aren't we dabbling in divine mystery when we attempt to come up with a 'spiritual' explanation for the accidental death of a high-spirited young girl, while a ninety-three-year-old man lies in a crowded nursing home almost unaware that his worn, emaciated body is being kept alive?" Price completely rejected the idea that God sends us trials in order to perfect us. She said that "to imagine God thinking up a masochistic trial in order to test me would drive me deeper into despair." The human problem is that "our hearts break, and we demand an answer." But along her faith journey, she learned that hope compensated for answers—hope and her trust in Jesus.

> Placing one's faith in Jesus in no way guarantees an insurance policy against smashed dreams or blighted expectations. The only direct statement of Jesus which is simple enough for me to comprehend when my heart is breaking or when I'm discouraged or scared is "Follow me." I cannot understand life because life is not understandable. But I can grasp "Follow me."

It is in that invitation that we find not answers, but a blueprint for our faith journey.

We can learn, too, from the wisdom of several rabbis who were interred in the Nazi concentration camps. The rabbis put God on trial and found him guilty. But then they realized they had passed judgment according to human standards, and they knew they had to submit these human standards to divine mystery. And so they prayed. You see, they knew God might have looked like a deadbeat Dad, but they trusted that he wasn't.

A parish priest once told me, when I was struggling with my faith, that we have to know Christ by faith because we cannot know him by history. He went on,

> And so we're back again to the question: how do you define

faith—or love, or hope, or truth or beauty? You can't define these unless you box them in. But can you really box in a mystery? There are no formulas for faith. A person comes into the community of faith through baptism. Through the Church growth in faith can be nurtured. But Christ's existence must become meaningful for each person individually. How this happens is the mystery of faith—which defies formula or definition.

One thing is for sure. Faith is not, and never has been, some kind of inert, protective device against the bad things in life, carrying a guarantee of heaven after life. Faith is a personal relationship with God. Like every personal relationship, faith must grow and thus be subject to all the crises, dangers, and adventures of life. And, like every personal relationship, it is wrapped in mystery, defying definition.

CHAPTER TWO

Endless Beginnings

Faith is not a thing which one "loses"; we merely cease to shape our lives by it. ▶ GEORGES BERNANOS

Some thirty years ago, I read a small book by Teilhard de Chardin called *How I Believe*. I remember being in shock when I read this admission from Chardin: "Certain though I am—and ever more certain—that I must press on in life as though Christ awaited me at the term of the universe, at the same time I feel no special assurance of the existence of Christ....As much as anyone, I imagine, I walk in the shadows of faith."

"In the shadows of faith"! How those words struck me. They expressed exactly where I so often found myself, not in the noonday sun of faith but in the shadows. I had been through a divorce, and I was raising and supporting my six children as a single parent. True, I would say I was not really a parent alone because I believed the Lord God was my partner and would not abandon me. But sometimes, when my emotions would get more dominant than my reasoning, I would feel totally alone.

My ex-husband had always taken long vacations by himself, telling me that the care and feeding of the children was my problem, not his, and sometimes I would sarcastically feel that my Godly partner was doing the same thing! But then God always had a way of putting me soundly in my place, letting me know he had not abandoned me at all. At these times my faith would break out of the shadows and I would know again, as Tolstoy put it, that "Faith is the force whereby we live."

I was asked once to give a keynote address on the topic "the faith journey." This stopped me in my tracks. That was it: we really are on a journey when it comes to faith. And this journey comes complete with detours and potholes, danger from others, narrow turns, winding roads, missing signs, and deceptive billboards along the way. We also make a lot of stops, requiring new starts if we are going to get back on this important journey. It became clear to me that not only I but most people get lost sometimes along this faith journey. And when this happens, all we can do—unless we choose to give up our faith—is begin again.

I started to liken these endless beginnings to my jumpy starts and stops each spring when I would get an annual burst of yearning to get my dormant muscles into shape. Every form of exercise would have great appeal for me and my fantasies would begin. I could see myself jogging, walking two miles a day, skipping rope every morning, and getting on with yoga exercises. But my planned spring ritual would always fail, and it was not too difficult to figure out why. It was because my scenario was unrealistic. The one good thing that always came out of this process was that I would try again regularly to get into some kind of fitness training. I called myself a "marathon beginner."

When I considered my new beginnings each year for a personal spring shape-up, I would always find a corollary on the spiritual level. I had to admit that I was a marathon beginner on that level too. (Comparing my spiritual progress with my physical training was not an original thought on my part. I stole it from Ignatius of Loyola, the founder of the Jesuits, who wrote a program called the Spiritual Exercises to help people on the journey to God.)

I remember confiding my miserable failures at shaping-up, both physically and spiritually, to a priest. He surprised me by confiding that he, too, had never gotten past the "warm-up" stage in following the Spiritual Exercises of Ignatius, which he described as the saint's training manual for making it successfully to "the better world." He pointed out, however, that he never rested on his failures, but always picked up and began again. He attributed this to, "in a word, my dear, faith."

As I grew older and became more aware of the faults and limitations in myself and in my world, I often remembered his use of the warm-up metaphor. It made me less self-deprecating when I could admit that I can at least keep myself at the warm-up stage in my training for heaven.

This revelation unfolded slowly, and was something of a shock to me. In my very young days, before I knew anything about the obstacles I would meet on my faith journey, I had set out to be a spiritual Olympic athlete. I determined that I would never choose money over principles, lash out at my children in anger, give in to temptation, be vain about my appearance, say no to those who needed me, and on and on. Needless to say, my record here has been one of regularly failing but beginning again.

As the years pass, the realization of imperfections in me and in the world have become clearer. Like the earth, I have my dry spells and my wet ones, my cold spells and my warm ones, my verdant times and withered ones, my growing seasons and harvests, my hurricanes and tempests, my dark nights and my days in the sun. I like to have my bed warmed by an electric blanket, discuss poverty over a full meal, sleep when I am tired, and read under the sun with a cool drink by my side. Still, I try to make people around me comfortable, recognizing the fun and absurdity in human existence, laughing with people, loving and praying with them— doing all of this while lightly grasping the goods of the earth in one hand and tightly grasping God's hand with the other. And sadly, I still falter, because neither I nor anyone else on the faith journey "has it made." We all fail; we all have to begin again.

Even after all these years, I am still in training, still doing warm-ups, tripping over reality, stumbling into human weakness, breaking down into selfishness, losing my grip now and then on what this life is all about. Yet I have not given up. I fail and get up and try again. I am a marathon beginner, still in the race. And this, I have come to understand, is the bottom line of faith—to never say, I give up, I've had enough, I can't take it, I can't make it.

God's VIPs

It is not hard to understand why we are always in danger of dropping out of the race. Our God can be confusing. God's ways are not such that we never again have to wonder who we are, why we are here, and where we are going. The faith journey does not have road maps, only a kind of wireless messaging that sometimes sounds like a lot of static. Our challenge is well stated by the great philosopher and writer Malcolm Muggeridge, a convert to the Catholic faith, who said: "Every happening, great and small, is a parable whereby God speaks to us, and the art of life is to get the message." Unfortunately, the message often gets blocked because we lose touch with our own importance, and this makes it hard to believe God wants to communicate with us.

Some twenty years ago, I was reminded what each of us means to God. At that point in my life, I felt my work and my parenting defined me, not my inheritance as God's child. One Sunday morning, I happened to catch a television program on problems facing the Catholic Church. The late Bishop Francis Mugavero of Brooklyn was answering questions about how church teachings were being confronted by the difficult issues of birth control, married clergy, women priests, gay Catholics, and remarried and divorced Catholics. In all his answers, this truly saintly man managed to inject a firm, loving, pastoral comment. Bishop Mugavero said that no matter what questions or difficulties come up, we were still talking about the very human people who make up the Church. He explained that he always emphasized to all his people, "In the eyes of God, everyone is a VIP."

The idea that each one of us is a Very Important Person to God was not original or new even back then. Yet when the Bishop spoke these words I felt as if I was hearing something terribly important for the first time. After several days of reflecting on his comment, I understood why I had been so affected by his statement. I had simply not thought of my individual importance to God for a long time. Frankly, I believe few of us give much thought to this.

Most of what we hear and do is not geared toward making us conscious of our individual importance and divine origin. Our culture, our world, our society has come to be characterized by bigness, speed, power. We can feel a bit like Lilliputians in a gigantic whirl where almost everything is spoken of in big numbers. Most of the time we appear to be only a small part of a moving whole, with the success of the big institution, the big industry, the big company the all important goal.

The bigger our world and our frame of reference, the more we appear to diminish. We become small, and in our time, being small is easily equated with insignificance. How can we, the small ones, be important when everything around us sends out the disturbing message that when you talk billions, you are also talking obsolescence and expendability? Here's an example: people today are not fired, as it was formerly called, but downsized. What a terrible word to apply to human beings, more proof we live in a world that shrinks the less "useful" to an ever smaller size.

When Bishop Mugavero said "In the eyes of God, everyone is a VIP," he turned me on. It was exactly what I needed to hear that day, that small is potent and is God's way of confounding the big and the mighty. We have divine evidence of this. There is the visible proof of our uniqueness in our faces, our personalities, our voices, our expression of thoughts. Our fingerprints are an extraordinary, personal signature, duplicated by no other living person. Tinier yet are the genes in our cells which program each of us to be absolutely different from every other living creature. To confound the mighty even further, God has created the mysterious microscopic world where, if left uncontrolled, single-celled creatures could fell nations by disease; where particles of atoms, seen only by the most perfected microscopes, contain secrets of the physical creation of the universe and of energy itself.

When you think of it, God really went overboard in giving us the message that small is potent. He knew, no doubt, that as the world grew into a giant, individuals could easily get lost in the bigness. Thus, God put in some controls to remind us that importance has nothing to do with size. The world may engulf us with its enormity and make us feel insignificant; but neither Madison Avenue nor Congress nor kings and sheiks can give us fingerprints. These come from God and are only one reminder that we are each one of a kind, so important that we rate this stamp of uniqueness.

Bishop Mugavero gave me an incredible gift that Sunday morning, one which made me stop in my busy tracks and get back on to my faith journey. With this joyful beginning I sang about how the world may make bigger and better technologies and institutions, but only God creates VIPs.

Yet we can't always find something inspiring like this to keep us solidly moving ahead on our faith journey. So many things can sidetrack us. One especially is the failure to see the riches God has given us and to trust that he made us to one day populate heaven. Nathaniel Hawthorne wanted us to see that "Our Creator would never have made such lovely days and have given us the deep hearts to enjoy them, above and beyond all thought, unless we were meant to be immortal."

Detours ahead

A bad trap to fall into is the "poor me" syndrome, where we fall off the faith journey and nurture self-pity like a second skin. Self-pity can happen to all of us now and then. Something triggers a disturbance inside us and all of a sudden we find ourselves concentrating on our deprivations. We mourn for what we don't have or for what we have lost, instead of exalting in what we do have.

Basic to our nature as human beings is the desire not just to have, but to have more. And so some people are chronic complainers, mired in self-pity, because they do not have what they think is enough. They suffer from a constant condition of subjective poverty. No one denies that objective poverty exists, where people have no shoes or running water, where they have shabby homes, scant food, poor education, and no health care. But subjective poverty is different. It is relative. It means feeling poor in relationship to others, feeling deprived because we don't have what someone else has, be it money, fame, good looks or good health.

We are poor proportionate to our expectation of what we think we should have, expectations which are determined by what is available to or possessed by others and not ourselves. When we concentrate on what we perceive are our deprivations, and don't bounce back to a balanced position by looking at all we have, then we can fall into self-pity, a hideous trap. I recall what Francis de Sales wrote, that the truly rich person is the one who is content with his possessions, not looking over his shoulder to see what other persons have and making comparisons.

Why is it so important not to fall into self-pity? That's easy to figure out. If we can't realize how rich we are simply because we are God's VIPs, we will have trouble staying on the faith journey because we are too busy focusing on ourselves.

Another detour that is all too common on our faith journey comes with setbacks, the times when the smooth ride gets bumpy or downright destructive, when our hopeful expectations get dashed to pieces. Once in a while we may have a week that makes us wonder if there is something to the belief that the stars temporarily rough us up!

I have had many of those weeks. Case in point: some years back, I attended a memorial service for a dear friend who had died at the age of ninety-two. After the service, I was the last one to leave the assembly hall. When I got to the parking lot, I found the rear of my car badly damaged. It was a classic case of hit-and-run. I knew right then and there that for the next few days I would be spending a lot of time getting the car repaired. But that was just the beginning of the week's problems.

In my job as executive editor of a weekly newspaper, I had been putting a lot of energy into hiring an assistant. The leading candidate for the job was a woman I knew to be a most capable newsperson. I made her a good offer, but to my dismay, she declined. I was back to square one in my search for a good worker. Then, to make matters worse, a coworker came back from vacation on crutches! I ended up working almost double time because with his injury, he couldn't put in the required hours.

One day during this dreadful week, in a frenzy over pressures to meet deadline, I ran out at lunchtime through pouring rain to grab a bite to eat. The driveway was wet and slippery. Being distracted and in a hurry, I slipped and fell, badly hurting my knees.

Well, the week went on like that. A coworker who was into astrology told me something about Pluto entering one of my houses—whatever that means. She warned me I would be in for a rough ride for the next three months. Thanks a lot. "Find a solid stake and hang on to it," she advised. I was happy that I wasn't a believer in Pluto's power.

Since I have always tried to rely on Christ-centered assistance to help me deal with trouble, I put aside the "bad stars" theory and uttered my usual prayer: I believe, Lord, but help my unbelief. Soon after, I started to see things in a different light. I realized that while it is normal to be upset over misfortune, sometimes we exaggerate our losses because they have messed up our expectations. For example, I had the expectation that I would leave the memorial service and have a peaceful, productive day; that the woman I liked would take the job I offered and make my life easier; that my coworker would come back from vacation refreshed and raring to go, not laid up with crutches; that I would go out and get lunch, not injured knees.

Most of us spend a fair amount of time and effort in planning our lives. We go about this with a kind of certainty that if step one is done, step two will follow. And if we plot or design a set of directions, our life will unfold neatly with the loose ends fitting into slots A and B. To convince us further that planning will make our lives go smoothly, we get advice from feel-good writers who challenge us to "take charge of your life" and "pull your own strings."

Yet we know that for all our planning, more segments of our lives go awry than we would like. The "best laid plans of mice and men" often get blitzed by happenings beyond our control—witness my very bad week. That is not to say it doesn't make sense to plan. Of course it does. It is both sensible and essential. But our expectations should include flexibility, tolerance, and adaptability for the inevitable times when rain falls on our parade. If we stay on the faith journey, the patience and the blueprints for mapping out our lives are there to discover in the life and words of Jesus.

Signs and scenery

There is always beautiful scenery along the faith journey, though sometimes we are so busy looking the other way that we fail to notice it. Recently, I was remembering some of the wonderful times when something I experienced made my faith soar like a crescendo in a great piece of music.

One of these touching moments happened years ago when my daughter Margee, then four years old, was very sick with a fever. My son Frank, who was two and a half, was quite upset that his sister couldn't play with him. I explained that she was sick, which made it hard for her to have the energy for play, hoping he could understand this. The next thing I saw gripped my heart. Frank had gone to his bedroom and gotten his blanket, the one he was so attached to that he wouldn't even surrender it to the washing machine. He went to his sister and placed his blanket over her, and I heard him say, "Now Margee, you'll get better." Did I have to wonder who had given this child the grace to have such empathy for his sister that he would share with her the one thing that sometimes seemed to be his very lifeline? Oh no. This was one of the times when God was very near, and my faith got an energy boost.

One of my grandchildren, Sophia, gave me another great lesson in faith. When she was six, Sophia asked her mother an interesting question. She wanted to know if she had been at her mother and father's wedding. My daughter Mary smiled and said, "No, Sophia. You weren't born yet." Sophia was quiet for a moment, then firmly corrected her mother. "Yes I was," she said. "I just hadn't shown up yet." Theologians tell us we have existed from all eternity in the mind of God. Sophia, of course, hadn't consulted with any of them. I think she had her own hotline to the Holy Spirit, and she sure revved up my faith that day.

I saw God quite clearly in a very unexpected place, on a bus in New York City, a place that has a reputation for being rough, crime-ridden, and uncaring. But this day, I saw a slice of life that made me believe goodness is stronger than meanness in people. It started when a physically disabled passenger got up to get off at his stop and dropped his transfer. With great difficulty, he tried to bend to pick it up. Immediately, three people stooped to help. The man managed a smile which said thank you.

On this same bus ride, I noticed an old woman sitting across from me who looked very grouchy. A smile never crossed her face. But when she got up to leave, she handed the bus driver a piece of candy. She told him she had heard him coughing and wanted to give him something to help his throat. I felt humbled. I hadn't even noticed the driver was coughing, but the woman I thought looked grouchy had noticed. She gave me a lesson in kindness.

Then a woman got on the bus and seated herself next to me. She started talking, saying she had just turned eighty, and that she was "a miracle." I thought, "Oh boy, I've got a live one here." How arrogant we can be sometimes. She went on to tell me that she had come to New York from Puerto Rico some forty years ago and had had a very rough life. She had nearly died from cancer, but her prayers and faith had saved her. By now I was listening. She gave me good advice about staying healthy and happy. Her formula: eat right, exercise, never give up, love other people, and stay faithful to God.

I wasn't just on a bus that day. I was on my faith journey, and had learned much about how we can see a world full of faith in action—if only we open our eyes and our hearts.

Sometimes the simpler the story, the greater the impact. I once saw a man and his wife in a garden where there were blueberry bushes. His wife was sitting on a bench while he picked berries. I watched as he separated the berries, all the very plump, ripe, sweetest ones going into one bowl, and the small ones in another. He brought the first bowl to his wife, and I'll never forget how he smiled at her, saying "These are the sweetest ones." He sat and ate the small ones. It was a simple deed of love but monumental, for this man had brought God into the garden.

I found another simple story that made me see God in a letter written by Walter Griffiths to the *Long Island Catholic* newspaper. Griffiths told of how he was doing some cast fishing one day. Next to him was a younger man, also cast fishing, whose line caught onto a large swan. The bird was upside down and clearly very frightened. The young man jumped off the dock into about three feet of water and started to reel in the swan. "He proceeded to gently pat the swan in the area of its head....To my surprise, the bird completely calmed down. This was really something to witness," wrote Mr. Griffiths. He continued,

> The man very methodically started to unwind the line while very gently talking and patting the bird. At the same time that the bird was freed, his tail was wagging. The young man was coming back to the dock when he turned around, went back to the bird, and whispered a few words and a few more pats to insure confidence....If the man had been wearing a white robe I would have thought it was God on the beach...for he did perform in God's light and Goodness.

Griffiths then asks, "Do you see God and goodness in people?" That is a question we should always ask ourselves. We might be surprised at how often the answer would be "yes." The world is full of people who are, as Fr. Robert Barron expresses it, "God's dialogue partners—participating in his work of creation" to bring to light how "God passionately loves the world that flows from him." We see faith every time we encounter God's goodness in others, the sign of a mysterious promise and power beyond us. These signs are given us, I believe, to help assure us that the anguish and sorrows which seem built into life are, in the long run, incidental to the perfect joy set aside for us and for which we were made.

Yet the question always comes back: why do bad things happen?—with an accent on "why?" Books have been written to help us understand this question, usually pointing out that this is not God's doing but simply the way things are in life. As for why God allows this, I don't have precise answers. I like to quote what a preacher named Joseph Hall once said: "I leave God's secrets to himself. It is happy for me that he makes me one of his court and not of his council."

One thing I have learned is that you cannot be faint of heart on the faith journey. You have to be passionate; the lukewarm never make it. You need soul and muscle strength to keep getting up and starting again when you hit the plaguing doubts. You need a passionate yearning to see the fun, the beauty, and the joy that are always there along the way.

There is a hunger in the human heart and spirit that cannot be filled by the products, the toys, the talk of this world. No matter how much we fight it, unless a person has hardened his or her heart into rock, the yearning periodically wells in us for something larger than ourselves—for a life made whole. This is the goal of faith. Alfred Lord Tennyson expressed that wholeness with these words:

Whatever ways my days decline
I felt and feel, though left alone
His being working in mine own,
The footsteps of his life in mine.

Looking back over decades of setbacks along my faith journey, followed by endless beginnings, I know now that it shouldn't take a genius to figure out why we hit the bumps and pits along the way. If everything were easy, we would never get to find out what powers we have or learn how to use them. If we never got uncomfortable, we would probably never ask for God, question what life means, or yearn for paradise. Setbacks can bear a gift for us. They can get us moving out of a comfort zone that would keep us locked into an ultimately deadly immaturity, blocking our connection to the God who made us VIPs.

CHAPTER THREE

When Darkness Persists

Jesus didn't come to this earth to scatter blessings and success among the faithful. He came so that everyone could find out what the Father is really like.

▶ EUGENIA PRICE

I remember a night back in 1976 when I sat listening to the swirl of the trees outside my window being shaken by one hundred mile-an-hour winds. For hours I had been hearing the hurricane warnings. Television reporters continually repeated the news that Hurricane Belle was expected to envelop central and eastern Long Island shortly before midnight. The storm was predicted to raise the tides of the south shore waters of the Island, and it was expected that homes might be washed away. People had been evacuated from the beach areas for their safety. I felt grateful that I lived in the center of the Island, twenty-five miles away from the north and south edges.

Having lived a long time on Long Island, I had already experienced hurricanes in the past, most of them mild but two of them severe. When a hurricane is severe, electricity can be out for several days, hot, downed wires can stretch across streets and houses, trees can fall on cars and houses and block roads. Hurricanes cause great disorder, much destruction, and sometimes death.

No wonder as I sat there listening to the crescendo of movement outside, I became increasingly uneasy. This feeling was a basic unrest that we all feel when we face an unknown situation with unpleasant possibilities—like being scheduled to undergo an operation, or getting news that you have been downsized, or driving to a hospital emergency room not knowing how severely ill or injured a loved one is, or being desperately lonely, or being in an accident, or getting a call from school that your child is in trouble.

This uneasiness is an offshoot of a basic fear that we may be hurt and lose some of our wholeness, or be rejected and lose some of our ego, all because of this unknown which is about to happen to us. Are we going to be hurt slightly, badly, moderately, or not at all?

As the rain started pouring like waterfalls, I became conscious of how nervous I was getting, even as two of my sons, then young teens, were finding the whole hurricane menace somewhat exciting. For them the idea of having an ordinary day whipped into an extraordinary one was a great way to shake up summer boredom. I mentioned that they might resent Belle a day from now if she stole our electricity and there was no hot water for showers. They laughed, and my thoughts took off again, telling me my boys shouldn't have to be afraid of phenomena like Belle until they were older. A great part of the beauty of youth is this innocence of suffering—there are exceptions, of course—which protects the young for a brief while from anticipating and understanding disaster.

The activity outside kept getting ever more intense, with thunder crashing and lightning making brilliant gashes through the sky. I heard a groaning, splitting sound out front. I ran to the window to see that my beautiful maple tree, planted by me and my son Frank eight years earlier, was stretched across our lawn. In its fall, the twenty-foot maple had hit and killed our red bud tree. I tried to visualize how the lawn was going to look with those two beloved trees gone, and I could only see the emptiness caused by their loss. Then suddenly, I was grateful. I could sense the hurricane moving away. I could relax now, and I thanked God that my children and I were safe.

I have come to think of us humans as being perpetually on a hurricane watch, although we are not aware of this until some drastic loss opens our eyes or makes us lose our innocence. Most times life goes on in a way we think of as "normal," when nothing extraordinary happens. Life is mostly smooth sailing. Times are good and we take it for granted that it is all going to stay this way.

Then the hurricane strikes, bringing a devastating loss. It leaves us in shock, our comfortable, controlled life shattered. Almost immediately we find ourselves empty, feeling an incredible loneliness. In this state, it is hard or even impossible for most people to feel kindly toward God. The "why?" questions take over. The faith that was once comfortable is now too shaky to support us. And yet without faith we are like non-swimmers in an ocean without water wings. Without faith, we are trapped in darkness.

The dark times have taught me to respect the simple routine of getting up, going to work, cooking for loved ones, and spending a quiet evening at home. I actually feel privileged when I can pray at night, "Thank you, Lord, for letting this be an ordinary day." I have also learned that the shaken faith periods are only temporary—unless you blind yourself to the ways God comes to help you. Most times he will look like a person, someone you know, perhaps, but it will be God.

Forever in my heart is the memory of a man who showed me God's face in one of my darkest times. He was the late Msgr. Gerald J. Ryan, auxiliary bishop of the Diocese of Rockville Centre, New York. I had met him in the early 1960s when he was the director of Catholic Charities and I was a reporter for the *Long Island Catholic*, the weekly diocesan newspaper. Msgr. Ryan was well prepared for his position, having earned an advanced degree in social work so he could minister more effectively to people in personal crisis. And that's right where I was at that time—in a personal crisis, struggling to maintain a family of six children while in a destructive marriage.

Msgr. Ryan suggested that my husband and I see a Catholic Charities social worker, and we did. Unfortunately, counseling only verified that separation was the only answer. This was a difficult decision for me and my children. As the situation at home deteriorated, I was advised to move out of the house temporarily with the children. My sister Jeannette, who lived two hundred and fifty miles away, took my children. I moved into a motel room in order to keep my job at the newspaper.

As soon as I moved into my motel room, I walked out to a nearby phone booth to call my office at the *Long Island Catholic*. The first message I had was from Msgr. Ryan, who wanted me to call him right away. And so I did. Msgr. Ryan had heard from my husband and wanted to assure me that Catholic Charities was there to help should the situation not be resolved soon. I thanked him. Then, unexpectedly, he asked me, "Toni, do you need money?"

It is hard to relate how that question affected me. In that moment it was as if I had heard Jesus' voice. Msgr. Ryan's incredible human concern for me hit a chord that touched me deeply. I found myself crying uncontrollably right there in that phone booth on Montauk Highway. When I finally was able to catch my breath, I thanked him and told him I thought I could manage. Nevertheless, Msgr. Ryan asked me to call him if I needed help.

I will never forget that moment or that priest. He had made me cry for the first time in more years than I could remember. I had always tried to be strong and optimistic, believing I should keep my pain to myself. I could not recall a time when anyone had cared enough about me to ask whether I needed anything. Msgr. Ryan's concern for me was so genuine and so surprising that he broke the padlock I had put on my emotions. I could be human and cry.

Never again would I doubt that Jesus is alive and well and among us, for I had felt his love come through this priest who took his commitment to be another Christ very seriously. I also felt assured that whenever my faith would be shaken again in the years ahead, God would come to hold my hand. I would just have to be alert enough to recognize him in whatever human disguise he would be wearing.

The paradox of loss

Few of us get through life without having to face difficult times. And it is hard to stand tall and feel confident in God's presence when the ground beneath us is rocking and shifting. Dr. Gairdner Moment, a biologist who served with the National Institutes of Health, once wrote that a chaplain at Johns Hopkins Hospital had told him that "Why me?" was the most frequent question he was asked by patients and their relatives. Dr. Moment continued:

> Such questions arise endlessly, as when a daughter is the only one of five teenagers killed in an auto accident; or when, in the prime of life, it is found that the head of a family has inoperable pancreatic cancer; or when a child, happy, loving, talented, is the one in a thousand to develop a devastating brain fever from a common childhood disease, or when a long wished-for child is born with hopelessly defective eyes. Such tragedies lay hold on the heart and refuse to let go. Yet they do not justify survivors torturing themselves.
>
> Of course life can never be the same after a tragedy, any more than it can be the same after a great joy. Those who do permit tragedy to poison the rest of their lives should read how one of the greatest of religious teachers expressed his acceptance of the universe.

Dr. Moment then went on to speak of Jesus, who gave no answer for the "Why me?" question but taught that no one is singled out for pain: "your Father in heaven...makes his sun rise on the evil and on the good, and sends rain on the righteous and on the unrighteous" (Mt 5:45).

This is a difficult paradox for anyone to accept, especially for those who have been baptized into the life of Christ. From a human perspective, we feel we deserve better from the God we acknowledge and worship. Pope John Paul II dealt with the paradox of loss back in 1996 when he was in Hungary, visiting elderly and sick nuns and monks at the Pannonhalma monastery. He said, "Illness is a paradoxical state. On the one hand, it is an impediment to the person, leading to the first hand experience of one's own limits and fragility; on the other hand it puts us in direct contact with the cross of Christ and opens new doors to us."

We could substitute any loss in place of illness—the death of a loved one, the end of employment, a bomb in an airplane—and the Pope's words would ring true. We all have to confront the fact that we are fragile and not in control of what can happen to us. Yet we are in control of how we respond. The Pope expressed the mystery of it all, that if we turn to Christ, somehow this pain, this loss, this cross, becomes a key to opening new doors to a joy we could never have imagined.

Some people face the paradox of loss head-on. One is Paula D'Arcy, who lost her husband and child in a car crash back in the 1980s. She wrote a book called *Gift of the Red Bird: A Spiritual Encounter*, in which she told of her continuing search for a faith that is stronger than anger, fear, and despair. She courageously went into the wilderness for three days, without food or books, to connect with God. While there, an unexpected storm came up, which she clearly saw as a metaphor for life. During the storm, D'Arcy hears God ask, "Paula, can you trust me even when you do not feel my presence? Can you believe when you do not understand my ways?" She writes,

That question overpowers everything. The storm within me becomes quiet and somehow I know that this is the question I have come into the wilderness to answer. What is greater, my fear or my faith? Do I want my own way, or do I really want God?...I've never experienced anything like the force of this raging wind. But God's question is posed with greater force. Who am I really? Am I his, or am I pretending?

And quietly, in the midst of the chaos of the night, I find a place of truth at the very core of me. I trust God. I sit for a long while in the silence of that knowing. If I blow away and die tonight, or live and am protected, I am equally safe.

I begin the walk back to my spot and (hopefully) my tent. I have been touched by a power and a tenderness which have thoroughly changed me. I know I must still look like me, but truly, I will never be the same. I walk slowly down the dirt path. I am new.

How deeply her words touched me. Paula D'Arcy found that the cross of Christ is a key that, as the Pope said, opens new doors for us. Loss moves us to seek what it is God wants of us, to trust that he loves us in spite of our not being able to understand his ways.

I have had many moments where God has given me the grace to accept all I have been given, the crosses as well as the joys. One powerful experience of Christ's love came the year after my son Peter died at his own hand. At the time, my faith truly was shaken because a beautiful, brilliant young man had suffered torment from something wrong in his brain cells for nearly eleven years, a pain so deep that he felt the only way out of it was to end his time on earth and "go home."

I had prayed and searched for a way to cope with the tormenting loss of my son. At times I wanted to scoff at a God who seemed to have abandoned my son and now me. In desperation, trying to find a way to hold on to my faith, I challenged God to lay a path before me that would shake the darkness out of me. Soon after, unexpectedly, I was invited to go to Oxford University in England for a summer program in religious studies. The trip offered a lifeline of hope, and I believed God had provided it.

The program was outstanding, and the companionship of the professors and my fellow students would be forever memorable. But God had more of a surprise for me. One morning, I felt strongly that I should take a walk, that I would find a church where I should make a visit. So I skipped class and went walking. There were a lot of churches in the area, but I felt drawn to one in particular. The main altar was in front of me as I entered the church. Then I noticed a Marian altar off to one side, a separate chapel devoted to the mother of Jesus which is commonly found in old churches.

The entire wall behind this Marian altar was covered by a raised sculpture of the Pietà, a depiction of Mary in agony, holding her dead son Jesus. I prayed intensely to Mary to help me. She had been there before me, holding a dead son to her heart. She knew the pain I was in; she had been pierced with the same torment. I felt she had a message for me.

Kneeling there, I closed my eyes. Suddenly I felt myself in a deep, dark pit, far too deep for me to get out of. My son Peter was on the ground above me. He was with Jesus, and they were dancing. They looked so joyful. I wanted so much to be with them. Peter knew. He came over to the edge of the pit and looked down at me. Smiling, he let me know that I could be up in the light with him and Jesus if I willed this strongly enough and if I believed him. Yes, yes, I told him. And then, immediately, I was with the two of them, bathed in light, so full of a joy that I could never describe.

I don't know how long this visualization lasted, but the joy of it will be with me forever. Never again would I ever wonder if God's mysterious ways are meant to hurt us. Indeed, the world hurts us but God is there to lift us out of our pits of despair and pain. That morning, I found a peace I believed would endure.

A year later, when I got the news that my son John and his wife Nancy had been murdered, that peace was tested. But because God had given me such a gift of grace that morning as I prayed before Mary's altar, I was able to hold on to his promise of peace even as I suffered the pangs of hell once again. I survived the agony of losing another son and a beloved daughter-in-law without falling into despair.

The miracle of love

Like myself, many people have found that love is bound up with eternal life. Some of them expressed their feelings in a very fine book called *The Courage to Grow Old*. William Nichols, who was editor of *This Week* for decades and a convert to the Catholic faith, wrote after his wife's death, "Let the theologians worry about the specifics of heaven and hell and the sex of angels. All we need to know is that the people we love—those deep in our memories and our hearts—are waiting for us there. Yet, at the same time, they are also with us here. This is the miracle. The miracle of love." I say "amen" to that.

Undeniably, some people stay locked in despair, focused on

life's limitations, blows, and restrictions. I once read an essay that saddened me. It was written by David Diamond, a twentieth-century composer then in his mid-seventies. He wrote:

I have been complex and melancholy. I remain so. This has made me uncertain of the future. The dead populate my memory's vast land of suffering and have therefore helped me live. But personal loss can also poison the soul. We gain little from losing those we have loved. We are made sorrowful. We are not ennobled by our suffering.

Diamond also acknowledged that music was what mattered most to him. Alfred Painter, a philosopher and Methodist minister, was the same age as Mr. Diamond when he wrote differently, optimistically, of life. His wife had died,

...deteriorating from the meaningless ravages of Alzheimer's disease. There could, after all, be no rational justification to account for such a tragedy...[but] what good would it have done me to ask: Why me? Why her? Why, God, did you allow this to happen? So rather than determine that life for me was over, I took the position that...there must be—simply must be!—some new course to follow.

Life is an endless adventure moved along by forces beyond our control, but one which we can give ourselves to in trust and confidence. There is always more going on than we are equipped to perceive through our limited senses and with our limited experience. The "more" is the root of religious or spiritual life. Change is at the bottom of it, and the more we are a part of it, the more we accept it, the more we rely and trust in it, the more likely we are to uncover the pleasures and mysteries of living.

Alfred Painter had discovered a rock-bottom essential for people who are dealing with troubled times, unexpected events, or shattered faith; that is, there is something more to be learned, someplace more to reach on our life's journey, a "new course to follow."

Margaret Elwell, a Pulitzer Prize-winning writer, told of her friend Nackey Loeb, "the woman who had everything"—until she emerged from a car accident a paraplegic, and shortly after became a widow when her husband died of cancer. With great courage, she took over the publication of her husband's newspaper, the *Manchester Union Leader*, and in the process found a new life for herself. When Elwell praised Loeb for her courage, she said, "But Margaret, what was the alternative?" Her friend knew that the choice was between "stagnation and death. Nackey chose life."

It doesn't always have to be a matter of life and death that puts us on a new course. I had a friend who was downsized from his job as a department store manager. Matt and his wife were devastated. They had recently bought a home, had a baby, and were in debt. It was a depressing blow for them, upsetting their plans and their progress. Matt was unsuccessful in finding a similar job, but the reason probably hinged on what he was communicating subconsciously to prospective employers. You see, he had hated his old job and only stayed with it because of his responsibilities to his family.

At one point a friend came along and asked Matt to work with him for a while. The friend made his living clamming off Long Island waters. Matt joined him and learned that he loved the freedom and natural environment of this work. He even earned more money than he had before. The job gave him time to go back to college and continue working in the health field, his strongest interest. Matt's "bad news" helped him to set a new course that turned his and his wife's lives around for the better.

I have met so many beautiful people who refused to be destroyed by a trauma that plunged them into darkness. In so many different ways, they chose life. One is Michael Barrett, who touched me deeply when he sent me a book he had written called *The Silent Stream*, reflective meditations that came from his soul. He had long suffered from the type of malady that tormented my son Peter, the illness they call manic-depression.

Michael grew up surrounded by sixty acres of woodland, and it was there that he literally absorbed the beauty of nature. As an adult, Michael kept going back to the woods. Time after time, surrounded by the beauty of nature, he found a healing that would endure. There he felt and rejoiced in the presence of God and the discovery of his own brightness.

The brightness of a day has little to do with whether or not the sun shines, or whether or not we have an electric lamp handy. No, our brightness is a measure of how transparent we are to the divine light whose rays consist of grace and peace beyond our understanding.

Michael said he put his reflections in writing so that people devastated by affliction "could find a voice that speaks to them." He told me, "Nobody is out there waltzing through the park." If everyone could understand the truth about how we can find the light that gets us out of darkness, as Michael has, their shaken faith would become strong faith.

In *Peace of Mind*, a book that has become a classic, Joshua Loth Liebman addressed the traumatic shake-ups that plunge people into darkness, leaving them fearful and faith-shaken. "Certain things we must endure, certain hardships and tragedies, defeats and losses, are part of our human destiny....The wisdom of life is to 'endure what we must and to change what we can.'" Liebman then gives a beautiful message of hope, one that may help us get back the self-esteem God intended for us regardless of how life batters us:

Master fear through faith—faith in the worthwhileness of life and the trustworthiness of God; faith in the meaning of our pain and our striving, the confidence that God will not cast us aside but will use each of us as a piece of priceless mosaic in the design of his universe.

CHAPTER FOUR

Grasping for Faith in Foxhole Times

For those who believe in Christ, there is no sorrow that is not mixed with hope—no despair. There is only a constant being born again, a constantly going from darkness to light.
▶ VINCENT VAN GOGH

Claudia Grammatico has become my friend, and shares her deep pain with me. On May 16, 1999, Claudia, her husband Paul, and their daughter Christine got the terrible news that devastates a family. Her son Paul, Jr., twenty-six years old, and a friend, Michael Penny, who was twenty-five, were fatally injured when a drunk driver slammed into their vehicle. Michael died instantly; Paul was brought to the hospital brain-dead, temporarily put on life support until his family could decide if they would donate his organs to patients in desperate need for these.

"My whole life spun out of control," Claudia told me. Her pain—and her faith—jump from the lines of the poetry she now writes:

My heart is broken with grief
  because I love you so...
  and grief has no symmetry,
  depth
  or height.

There is incredible Holiness
  in my heart's affections.

I detest being stuck in the Outpost of Absence.

This is a Sacred Path.

Indeed, from the moment of Paul's death, Claudia took the difficult, sacred path her son would have chosen, donating his organs to give the gift of life to others. Paul "lives" in nine people who had been fatally ill. His heart now beats in the chest of a Long Island man; his liver was given to a woman in New York; one of his kidneys was transplanted in a woman from Kansas with three children, the other to a man in Nevada with two children; a lung went to a nurse in Massachusetts; his bone will help heal children with spinal and joint deformities; and his skin aided burn victims needing grafts.

Claudia now calls herself "donor Mom" and is on a mission to educate people on the importance of organ donation. She says that giving Paul's organs to others "made all the difference in how I cope as well as in how I go on with my life." This Catholic mother says that she, too, is a "transplant recipient, with a new heart and spirit to be of service to others in their trauma, sorrow, and transformation." She truly is a woman of faith.

And yet, Claudia sends me e-mails that are wrenched with torment, and I feel her tears. For she has learned, as do all people who lose a loved one, that the pain never goes away. She is in a foxhole, as her words affirm: "I knew in a moment that the cup of misery would not pass and the pit of death was bottomless." But she is not alone in that dark place because she holds on to her trust in God's promise of eternal life.

I recall here the famous line that came out of World War II:

"There are no atheists in foxholes." For when disaster is imminent, when earthly securities dissolve, when our feeble attempts to mask life's fragility fail—that is when the stirring starts inside us, drawing us to look beyond ourselves and reach out for a reality that can make some sense of our lives. Some of us give that reality a name: "God."

It has long been known that when people experience disaster, many turn to God. In times of catastrophes such as floods, hurricanes, tornadoes, and volcanic eruptions, even those of no faith often "rediscover" God. This happened after the nuclear accident at the infamous Three Mile Island plant in Pennsylvania, in March of 1979. A team from Rutgers University surveyed people who lived in the affected area. Its findings, carried in *Psychology Today*, revealed that forty-three percent of the 359 homeowners within a twenty-mile radius of the plant said the accident had increased their faith in God. The researchers called this a "religious fallout."

In that story, *Psychology Today* quoted one of the investigators, James Mitchell, as saying, "When catastrophic events such as this occur, they (the people affected) look to God to guide and sustain them. In fact, they may have attributed the absence of death and destruction to God's divine intervention."

I was not surprised when I read that nearly half the people close to Three Mile Island turned to God. They had to face the very real possibility that their food could be contaminated and the air they breathed laced with radioactivity, that the water they drank could become an ion-cocktail, that the babies they bore could be damaged before birth. They felt panic at not being in control of their lives. These people knew what it meant to be in a foxhole.

I have heard people scoff at those who turn to God in times of disaster. God isn't going to help or make a difference; you make the difference for yourself, they say. If you believe God is helping, their argument goes, what has actually happened is that you have helped yourself by your positive assertions—and then given God the credit. My reaction to this kind of explanation is that it is sophisticated nonsense. Real faith and trust in God has no resemblance at all to self-hypnosis. But to understand this and to believe this, it is necessary to have been in a foxhole with the world exploding around you—and most of us *have* been there.

Foxholes come disguised in many shapes and are found in so many different situations. They look like hospital emergency rooms, divorce courts, fires, floods, diseases, famine, hospice facilities, shelters harboring victims of violence, homes shared with alcohol and substance abusers, revolutions, hijacked planes, embassies with hostages, nuclear power plants spilling poisons of unknown quantities and consequences, and on and on.

Some people trapped in a foxhole adjust to the darkness; some despair; some turn to God. Those who choose God do not do so out of cowardice or weakness or as a form of escape. They turn to God motivated by a faith that simply and clearly acknowledges the limitations of the human condition and the unlimited power of the Creator.

I have been in many foxholes. One of the scariest ones was the time when my brother Joe was afflicted with hairy cell leukemia and given six months to live. I was eight years old when Joe was born, and he was the first person in my life who stirred a new emotion in me that I later learned was love. I wanted to take care of him, protect him, show him off so he would be noticed. I would comb his golden curls so everyone could marvel at his beauty, as I did. When he had scarlet fever at age seven, I cooled his cheeks with mine and never worried about the contagious germs. The first creative writing I ever did was at age nine, when, inspired by my baby brother, I wrote an ode to him. Now that he was ill, I could not bear to think of a world without my beloved brother.

I have seven brothers and sisters. When Joe was diagnosed as being fatally ill, the bond among us became stronger as we turned, united, to God. We learned that in the isolation of the foxhole, the distance between us and God closes. It is clear that in these times, when we are overwhelmed by our mortality, the only logical place to turn for help is to our Source, to the One who gave us life. And so as a family we humbly prayed for a miracle—and we got one. In the hands of God and baffled doctors, especially with the good care of his physician, Dr. Frank Lizzi, my brother has survived his leukemia for twenty-eight years, as of this writing. We don't try to explain this because no language exists to explain mysteries.

In foxhole times, you don't worry about being smart, sensible, powerful, logical, or anything earthly. You are too enveloped in the ending-side of existence, and so you yearn for the unending—God. You do, that is, if you have faith.

A tested faith

As my life went on I found myself in ever more foxholes, often desperately hanging on to faith. During these times I found consolation in knowing I had much in common with Jesus—like carrying a very heavy cross.

My father had arranged a marriage for me when I was nineteen. This was the custom in southern Italy where he came from, and there was no arguing about it. Nor was there a courtship. (I think this was to insure that virginity remained intact!) I was alone with this selected man for the first time only after the vows and the celebrations were over with. In the painful years that followed, I often asked the Lord: could this have been called a real marriage? But being a good Catholic, I never considered divorce until I saw my children being harmed. And so in 1967, I became a single parent, raising and supporting my six children alone. (I also have an adopted son, who by that time was out on his own.) It was a tough life but a good life, in spite of the few foxholes I fell into.

The good life turned sour when I lost two of my sons. In 1991 my youngest son, Peter, committed suicide. He was afflicted with the onset of a chemical disorder in his brilliant brain when he was seventeen years old. That marked the beginning of his ten-year struggle to have a life. During that time he achieved so much—a successful two-year tour in the Army, a *cum laude* college degree, a job teaching in a high school, and three books published by major houses. But his condition kept getting worse, and Peter believed that it was time to "go home," as he put it in notes he left. He went to a pond where he used to sit and meditate, and put a bullet through his head. I descended into an indescribable foxhole.

Then, two and a half years later, came a shocking phone call telling me that my son John and his wife Nancy, who had recently moved to Montana, were dead—murdered. It was four months before the murderer confessed. He turned out to be the eighteen-year-old son of the people from whom my kids had just bought their home, with the strange name of Shadow Clark.

When I heard Clark's account of the crime, I thought I would die. I could see him breaking silently into the house where he had lived since he was three. He knew every inch of it, how to sneak up the stairs without a sound. I have a nightmarish vision of seeing him standing there at two in the morning, with his 9mm automatic gun aimed at my sleeping son's head. One shot killed John instantly. Nancy wasn't so lucky. She was awakened by the explosion and reached for her glasses. I cannot imagine what she went through at that moment when she saw what was coming. She went into a fetal position and he shot her twice.

If ever faith is tested, it is in dark times like these. Stuck in a foxhole, I had to get to the gut reality of what I really believed when the God I had come to love and trust would allow such pummeling to attack my heart, my very being. What kind of a relationship did we have anyway? I kept asking the Lord this question—and I began to learn.

I first had to acknowledge that the key to an honest relationship is to let the other be who the other is. Relationships break because we try to remake someone else according to our own blueprint. As I listened to myself scream at God, I realized what I was really protesting was that he hadn't lived up to what I had expected of him. I berated God for not giving me the life I thought I deserved.

When I was a teenager, I remember sitting on a bus listening to two older women talking. One was telling the other about her boyfriend who wanted to marry her. She wasn't sure, she said, talking loudly. She had her conditions. "I'll take him for better, but not for worse." That is the human way. We want to hedge our bets. We want others to conform to our specifications, our images. And we do this with God, too.

We ask and pray for things, and when we don't get them we scream at God. We don't let God be who God is—the wondrous

Mystery, the One who promised "I am always with you," the One who continually brings the universe into being, the One who does not arbitrarily change the laws that govern creation, the One who gives us everything but answers. Augustine said, "If you understand, it is not God that you understand." This great Father of the Church explained that we must leave room for God's freedom, and that the worst assumption we can make is believing we human beings know how and why God works.

We want God to be like some cosmic bellhop bringing us what we ask for. When he doesn't cater to our requests, we end the relationship and say, "I've lost my faith." Yet loss can teach us that life doesn't come with answers, and so we must grapple with mystery. Suffering forces us to the threshold of mystery. I have learned that if we cannot accept mystery, we are stuck in our pain. We cannot heal. I can relate to what Robert Hater said in his book, *The Search for Meaning*: "Suffering takes us to a core mythic meaning. Speculation about suffering raises questions that point to an ultimate realm of existence, deeper than one can fathom, which holds the final secret to life's mystery." No wonder pain and suffering have been called the seeds of awakening.

After the deaths of my sons, I searched all over for help with my pain, going to lectures, reading recommended books, going to monasteries to pray. I found myself drawn to the Book of Job. His story tells of the most fundamental question of life's journey: why this suffering, and who is this God that started everything we are, we have, we see?

Most people know the story of Job, how he was a good man who had everything taken away from him—wife, children, possessions, and health. He experienced so much misery and loss. Many people would ask me, "Don't you feel like Job sometimes?" My answer was yes, but if I used the Job analogy to describe my loss, I would have to do more than shake my fist at God. I would have to listen to God's response to Job's complaints, given in words that are sheer poetry:

I will question you, and you shall declare to me...Where were you when I laid the foundation of the earth? Who laid its cornerstone when the morning stars sang together and all the heavenly beings shouted for joy? Have you commanded the morning since your days began, and caused the dawn to know its place? Do you give the horse its might? Do you clothe its neck with mane? Is it at your command that the eagle mounts up and makes its nest on high? (Job 38—39)

God is telling Job that there is a colossal mysteriousness to the created realm. He is telling Job to accept alluring mystery and berating creatures who dare to imagine they can understand the ways of God. But does this make God a monster of unpredictability and arbitrary acts? I don't believe so. God's response shows how God literally revels and rejoices in all he has created—especially us. God passionately loves the world that flows from him. And God invites Job into a warm and personal encounter with himself.

If we get to know Job's God, we can form a new vision of what life and faith really are. The first thing we learn is that our lives are not solely about us, but about a power and a promise beyond us. To have faith is to be overwhelmed by the reality of God, absorbing the divine energy he so generously gives us. Thomas Aquinas said that God is always at work at the very roots of our being. God wants us to participate in his life, but we are built ultimately for listening and for following, not for commanding.

When we read Job, we get a sacramental view of the universe. Ours is an enchanted universe where the divine is at play. In his book, *And Now I See...*, Fr. Robert Barron writes, "Even the whales in the depth of the ocean are Divine accomplices—agents of the sacred—that allow the world to be what it is—a theater for the glory of God." Why God designed this world to have so much death and rebirth is not for us to know, but certainly he wanted us to fully enjoy his theater.

Famed biologist Dr. Gairdner Moment saw this clearly.

Is a lily for a day worthless? Should sunsets be canceled because even the most glorious don't last forever? Each snowflake is unique in its loveliness; its life spans but an instant of a circling year, yet it bears the imprint of eternity.

Learning to see

We don't see the enchantment of the universe when we are in a foxhole, but only its limitations and imperfections. What then becomes most important for hurting people, myself included, is to get to the place where we can forgive God for all the suffering and pain in this world—essentially, forgive God for making an imperfect world.

Yes, God made an imperfect world. Why? I don't know. That is in the realm of mystery. If we go back to Genesis, the words, "In the beginning..." let us know that God did not give us a ready-made world. He got it started, and when he made human beings he said, "Go!" From the beginning, we have been co-creating the world with God—and therein lies the problem with imperfection.

God put the progress of creation into our hands—us, his people, who bungle things quite easily. We see that every day. Everything in nature could be said to have a bungling side because creation wasn't made perfect—or finished. No wonder there are pitfalls and cliffs and rocky places and horribly evil humans and all the rest of creation that brings pain and loss into the world and into our lives.

The gift of divine love was that God gave his creatures independence from the very beginning. But this is also why we have disasters—like a gun in the hands of an eighteen-year-old who blew away the earthly lives of two fine people, my children. Even something like cancer, which occurs when cells go wild, is the downside of a yet imperfect world creating itself.

Clearly, the universe was never God's puppet theater, with God a divine puppet master pulling the strings. The God of love could not be such a cosmic tyrant. Yet that is what we have made of him. That is why we keep asking, why does God let bad things happen to us? Why doesn't he interfere and make everything great for us? Now, none of this brings any comfort when we are stuck in our foxholes, each facing our own human suffering. But all I am trying to do here is to give some insights into the profound mystery of human suffering: insights, not answers. And when I think of creation this way, I see God differently. He isn't up in heaven somewhere, pulling our strings; God is with us when things go bad.

Once in meditative prayer, I asked my late son Peter why we have to suffer so much pain. He didn't really answer but he communicated something I will never forget: "God suffers your pain with you." Imagine that! I remember once having read about Holocaust victims who were asked, "Where was God when this crime against you happened?" And some answered, "He was there suffering with us."

Kierkegaard, the nineteenth-century Danish religious philosopher, understood that God identifies with our suffering. He wrote, "There is no remembrance more blessed, and nothing more blessed to remember, than suffering overcome in solidarity with God; this is the mystery of suffering." And William Blake, the eighteenth-century poet, wrote a most touching poem which echoes this sentiment:

Think not thou canst sigh a sigh,
And thy maker is not by;
Think not thou canst weep a tear,
And thy maker is not near.

O! He gives to us his joy
That our grief he may destroy;
Till our grief is fled and gone
He doth sit by us and moan.

I am convinced that pain is wrapped in a spiritual challenge. Isn't it right that at some point, most of us recognize that even though pain has crushed us, altered us, and reshaped us we still hold the power to be stronger than our pain? We can stay strong because God's grace is always there for us to tap into, just for the asking: "Ask and you will receive" (Jn 16:24).

I have learned that with God by your side, suffering can lead you to take charge of your life. You will never be the same, but now you can see that you don't want to be who you were before you descended into the foxhole. You have been transformed. Maybe now you have found a compassion and understanding for others that you never knew was in you before. Maybe now your heart has been so softened by pain that you have nothing but empathy for others, which more and more becomes a radical love for them. The lessons you have learned from suffering have not brought you back to the pre-pain person you were; they have brought forth a new person. That is the mystery of suffering, and the promise so well expressed by the apostle Paul: "So if anyone is in Christ, there is a new creation" (2 Cor 5:17).

The miracle we can see every day is that we have life, that God has given us what only he can give. Yet he gives us this life with no guarantees on time—or anything else earthly, for that matter. God only gives us the promise of finding our real home, heaven, putting us on notice that to locate the route we have to follow his complex, mysterious blueprint. And I believe God wants us to discover that not only the destination but the trip itself is more than worth the effort.

CHAPTER FIVE

Forgiveness Is Faith's Command

Hatred never ceases by hatred, but by love alone is healed. This is the ancient and eternal law.

▶ BUDDHA

A woman called me in tears which I thought came from sorrow—until she started talking. She immediately expressed furious anger at another member of her family because of a trust betrayed. She had told her sister something in confidence, and the information had become known to everyone, the topic of conversation for a week on busy telephones. She felt justified in crying her tears of fury.

Unquestionably, she had been treated unjustly by her sister, who should have respected her privacy. Yet instead of trying to clear the air and heal the damage, this woman was locking up her anger, declaring, "I'll never forgive her for this, nor will I forget it."

I have heard those words so often, and seen what happens to

people who can't let go of the pain of having suffered an injustice. They let something from the past pollute their present and they don't even realize how they are being damaged by this, both psychologically and spiritually. Even as far back as Confucius, the wise knew that "To be wronged is nothing unless you continue to remember it."

Forgiving someone who has hurt us is one of the hardest things to do, given our human nature. Forgiving is alien to us who love to get revenge and even the score. Yet one cannot claim to be a person of faith, cannot bring a gift to the altar of God, without first undergoing the cleansing that requires us to be reconciled with our neighbors.

I have spent a lot of time in the past decade rereading the gospels and it has become clear to me that the bottom line message of Jesus was "forgive." He didn't come to sprinkle holy water on the world's status quo. He was a rule breaker, offering—rather, mandating—new rules for humankind that were virtually incomprehensible. His words generated sneers from a lot of people, from the powerful and comfortable who liked their power but also from the miserable and oppressed who liked their hate. His new rule was "love everybody." Was he out of his mind? "Forgive everybody?" Impossible! Of course it was—because Jesus was trying to give birth to a new earthly society, one his Father wanted, qualitatively different from the one rooted here.

G. K. Chesterton, an English writer and convert to Catholicism, didn't pull any punches about how mistaken anyone was to think that "God is in his heaven and all's right with the world." To set things right, he said, God had "to leave his heaven" and take on human skin, a human face, and a human voice. "Christ has made it possible for every man to reach the vision of God," said Thomas Aquinas. To think about this, really focus on it, is mind boggling. For it means that each of us individually can know God and see what he wants of us by absorbing the blueprint Christ laid out for us during his life. The staggering message of the New Testament is that we become one with God by becoming a clone of Jesus.

Sad to say that in the past, the Christian churches haven't always been clear about this message, being more fixed on sin than on love and forgiveness. When I was over in England for the summer program at Oxford, one of our professors was the Rev. Richard Holloway, bishop of Edinburgh. He was a genuinely human and honest man. At the time he was working on a book he called *Anger, Sex, Doubt and Death*, writing it, he said, because he saw these areas as the four major challenges facing Christians.

Bishop Holloway felt that the Christian denominations had become coated with "unhealthy attitudes that continue to disfigure the Christian community." Being so law-based had given rise to hardness of hearts, along with a tendency to judge people as sinners instead of beloved children of a God who is always merciful. In doing so, Jesus, who knew the human heart and looked at us with compassion, could be so easily overshadowded and his words—God's words—drowned out.

The bishop wanted to change this situation, so he was promoting the crucial need to preach and teach God's true message. He said it was his "increasing conviction that the Christian gospel, beneath the moralistic accretions that have characterized it, is about the unconditional grace and forgiveness of God." If ever we needed to be convinced of this, all we had to do was remember Peter and the cock crowing. "Peter's story," he said, "encapsulates the pure essence of the Christian message, which is that we are accepted by God even at the moment of our deepest betrayals."

The words Jesus most often spoke were of mercy and forgiveness. If there was anything that made Jesus stand out, it was that he preached a message of forgiveness "so revolutionary that organized Christianity has found it almost impossible to live with," as Bishop Holloway put it. The same is all too often true for individuals, especially if they have been deeply hurt and point their wrath at God for not preventing whatever it was that happened to them, be it the death of a loved one, the loss of a job, a hurricane, physical illness, and so on.

Yet Jesus couldn't have been clearer about where we must stand when it comes to forgiveness. Even the prayer to our Father that he left us, the one repeated by Christians of all denominations for centuries, emphasizes this: "Forgive us our trespasses as we forgive those who trespass against us." As Jesus went from crowd to crowd, he constantly spoke of ending hate and planting love. No more "an eye for an eye," no more revenge. You must love your enemies and pray for those who hurt and persecute you. You must forgive seventy times seventy times seventy, *ad infinitum*. And Jesus went to his death still preaching forgiveness, even of his executioners who, he wanted us to understand, did not know what they were doing.

If ever there was a hard lesson to digest it is this one: we must forgive others whatever hurtful deeds they do to us. Jesus told us that if we did this, we would overcome evil with good. But it takes great faith to accept this statement when we see that evil has a power capable of destroying us. I could feel considerable empathy for the Catholic woman, who like myself is the mother of a murdered son, when she told me "If faith means I have to forgive that murderer, then all I have to say is, that is an impossible command. I can't, I won't forgive."

Confronting forgiveness

After I lost one son by suicide and another by murder, I had to make a choice. I could cave in to my anger and despair, or I could seek to find the peace that would let me get on with life. It was a formidable challenge and a crucial one, for I knew that more than my mental and emotional health were at stake. So was my faith, the anchor that kept me convinced I had a relationship with a loving Father—not with a deadbeat Dad.

On a Tuesday night in December, 1993, I faced the beginning of the period I have come to call the moment of truth in my life. Homicide detectives had found the person who had murdered my son and daughter-in-law four months earlier. Where did I stand on forgiveness now that the murderer had a face and a name?

That night, Joe Geldrich, sheriff of Lake County, Montana, called me. "I have some news for you," he said. "We caught the murderer of your son and daughter-in-law." The news which followed stunned me. The killer, he said, was the eighteen-year-old son of Mr. and Mrs. Joe Clark, the people from whom John and

Nancy had bought their home only a few months earlier. His name was Joe "Shadow" Clark and he was a first-year student at a Quaker college in Oregon. They found Shadow, the name he was known by, because he had started talking to some fellow students about having killed two people. The students reported this to the school administrators, who then went to the police.

I kept interrupting the sheriff, wanting to know why this boy—who he called "an honor student and a fundamentalist Christian"—had killed my kids. But Joe Geldrich didn't know. Shadow Clark never said why, not then or afterward. As the case turned out, he entered a plea bargain and got life imprisonment with no parole until he is sixty years old. Throughout, he never revealed his motive for killing two beautiful people.

Never did I feel my faith so challenged as it was on that December night, my heart severed and bleeding. Now I was in a new place, facing a raw confrontation with my soul. I had been confronting the words of Jesus, that we must forgive those who do us harm, ever since I got the dreadful news about the murders. I had always been able to forgive those who hurt me in the past. But this was different. This person had killed my son and daughter-in-law, and had seared me and my remaining five children with a pain that would endure forever. Now I had his name and could see his face. Could I forgive him?

Someone once said, "The death of a child is an impossible grief," and that is so true. It puts you in real danger, in a place where your pain gets ferocious enough to take over and literally eat the goodness out of you. I would tell myself that I was the one in charge of damage control. The pain couldn't stop me from growing, working, and loving unless I let it. I was the one with the choice. If I stayed bitter and angry, I would give my pain the power to destroy me.

If I was to stay true to my faith, I would have to say, "Father, forgive him for he didn't know what he was doing." I would have to believe, as Jesus said, that evil is overcome by good. But, in gut honesty, now that the question of forgiveness would never again be academic or simple for me, could I say, "Father, forgive the murderer of my beloved children?"

This was a most disturbing question. For many weeks, it surged up through my prison of anger, pain, desolate sadness, and beautiful memories of John and Nancy. It frightened me. The uncertainty of where I was and how I could come to an answer put me in a bleak place. I wondered if I would become hardened by this brutal crime, even as I remembered the plea from Psalm 95, "Do not harden your hearts."

I started to meet with other victims of crime, asking if they could forgive the one who had hurt them. Most of them couldn't get over the anger. As I listened, I realized why they wanted to remain angry. Anger made them feel powerful; it was their weapon poised at the criminal. Some expressed the fear that to forgive would mean they were weaklings, soft on criminals. I could see what some of them couldn't; that their anger was keeping them locked in hate, eroding them. When I would turn on the television news and hear about the killings and retaliations among the Serbs and the Muslims in Bosnia, and the Arabs and Jews in Israel, I would strongly feel that I was hearing the same message: we hang on to hate to feel powerful. It was all so wrong, and so contradictory to the message of Christ.

I read about a mother whose daughter was killed by her husband. Her son-in-law was now in prison, and had written to her to say he had "found Christ." Unable to forgive him and in anguish, the mother told her minister that she felt the killer would go to heaven and be with her daughter, while she would be in hell because she could not forgive him. I shuddered, realizing the devastation this woman had brought upon herself by not being able to forgive.

Even as I was struggling with my personal loss, I could see more and more what happens to people who can't let go of their pain from having suffered an injustice, and how they become damaged psychologically and spiritually. I didn't want to choose that fate.

After getting the horrible news of the murders, I had wondered if I would become hardened by this brutal crime. I prayed, and the Lord helped me to understand a new slant on forgiveness, how it has a spotlight effect, revealing who we really are when we become the victim of brutal evil. I was not to fall into the pit of letting this sword of sorrow erode my soul with hatred or a desire for revenge.

Yet it is so natural, so human, so easy to let hurts take root in us and crowd out our hearts. We have been socialized to value revenge, from the "cowboy and Indian" movies we saw as kids to the constant wars fought throughout the world and the current pro-death penalty bandwagon rolling across the country. Forgiving one who has hurt us is one of the hardest things to do, given human nature. I can recall my father's Italian friends who would say that forgiveness is not a sign of weakness; it means you have a strong soul. Yet in practice, if anyone hurt them they would "even the score," to use their words. We want an eye for an eye because that makes us feel powerful. We blind ourselves to the truth that, as Carl Jung said, "You always become the thing you fight the most." In other words, we become what we hate.

I saw this clearly in a movie released in early 1996 called *An Eye for an Eye*, starring Sally Field, who played a mother whose daughter is raped and murdered. The system fails the mother by letting the murderer get off on a technicality, and so the mother goes for revenge. She gets a gun and learns to shoot so she can kill the man. Those responsible for this film had one thing in mind: to push the hate buttons in all of us, and it worked. At the end of the movie, when the mother pumped bullets into the rapist, everybody in the theater was hooting and hollering and clapping for the mother, who had now become a murderer herself.

I later saw Sally Field on the Oprah Winfrey television show, where the hostess asked the actress if she had come to empathize with the mother. Ms. Field said no. The mother, she said, goes down into herself and touches the dark places there, the latent evil that can always haunt us. She descends to become what the killer is. I admired Ms. Field for her insightful understanding of the evil of revenge. But I don't think the movie audience shared this insight. They were force-fed the false power of revenge, an eye for an eye, and cheered for violence.

I had long been praying that the sword of sorrow with which Shadow Clark had pierced me would not erode my soul with hatred or a desire for revenge, and the Lord was hearing my prayer. After seeing the Sally Field movie, I understood that forgiveness must begin deep in my gut and in my soul.

My personal life had become a battleground, but I kept praying. I looked into my soul and found God's footprints there. We all have his footprints on our souls, and they have a name: grace, a gift that never fails so long as we accept it. Grace is ever there to remind us where we came from and to help us get unlocked when we are in conflict. It is there as we struggle with our feelings when we become the victim of brutal evil or of lesser crimes, like assaults to our ego. I knew God's grace was with me to strengthen my faith and bring me peace.

Unlocking the hurt

I have seen people stay locked into hurt from all kinds of injustices, both perceived and real. But I have also seen nobility shine from a person after severe hurt and loss, like Debbie Morris.

In 1998, Debbie wrote a book called *Forgiving the Dead Man Walking*. Many people are familiar with Robert Willie because his story had been told by Sister Helen Prejean in the book *Dead Man Walking*, which was later made into a movie. But not many people know about his other victim, whose name was not revealed till long after the trial. Debbie was sixteen when she was abducted by Willie and Joseph Vaccaro, his partner in crime. At the time, they were being pursued by police for the murder of young Faith Hathaway. Willie repeatedly raped and terrorized Debbie and probably would have killed her but for what she believes was divine intervention. The two men were captured, and Willie, who got the death penalty, was executed on December 28, 1984, four years after Debbie's ordeal.

When she told me her story, I felt her pain. I could understand why she had gone into an acute depression, and experienced alcohol abuse and physical weakness. She also felt hostility not just toward Willie, but also toward people whom she felt had no empathy for what she had gone through. Debbie was on an agonizing road when one day she felt drawn to enter a church. Immediately she felt such joy, she knew it had to have been God who had led her there. She realized her despair had come from being stuck in self-pity, and that she had blamed God for allowing her to suffer so much at such a young age. She said,

I understood then that God didn't cause the kidnapping to happen to me. True to his laws, he didn't interfere with Willie and Vaccaro. He allowed them to exercise their will. I knew then that I had forgiven God, and because of that, God could use me to make good things happen.

The night Willie was executed, I didn't feel anger any more. I surprised myself by telling God "I really do forgive Robert Willie." When I said those words, I felt a sense of freedom hard to describe. By wanting to forgive this man who treated me so badly, I cut myself free from the control he had over me. Now I knew I needed to forgive for a much bigger reason. I needed to forgive in order for me to receive forgiveness. I had to pray for Willie because he is a child of God and God loves him the same as he loves me. He wants him in heaven as much he wants me. Once I realized that, and understood it meant I had to love as Jesus did, I had no choice but to forgive. If we once understand this and live in defiance of this, we can't have peace.

Debbie's faith warmed and astounded me, especially as she went on,

I used to wonder why I had to suffer so and why God kept me alive. Now I know the answer to both. I received God's comfort and now I am to take what I have received and give it to others. Live with forgiveness and grace. That's the message I want people to hear.

Mostly I want to help others feel the tremendous power of forgiveness. For a long time I had put an emphasis on the hope that when Willie was executed, I would have a sense of peace and closure and normalcy restored to my life. I thought I would be healed. But the day after the execution I realized

I was numb. Nothing was different except that a man was dead. I think when you're looking for justice, healing, and peace of this magnitude, you need to look to a higher authority, and that's Our Lord. Justice hadn't healed me. Forgiveness did.

Debbie affirmed what I had long seen, that there is a paradox when we talk of forgiveness. It is this: we cannot heal if we do not forgive others. But if we do forgive, then it is we ourselves who benefit the most.

Shortly after I received the news that my son's murderer had been found, I got a call from a reporter asking me how I felt about the murderer. I responded instinctively, with two words: "incredibly sad." That is when I knew I had begun to forgive. I was utterly saddened to think of an eighteen-year-old who had permanently altered so many lives and destroyed three, John's, Nancy's, and his own. I had started to pray for Shadow Clark, that he could respond to God's grace and be redeemed. All this did not help me to understand why there is evil in the world, nor did I have any new answers for why terrible things happen to us and those we love. As Bishop Holloway would often repeat in his classes, "We find ourselves thrown into a universe that comes without an explanatory leaflet attached." But I was learning I had the power to forgive, and that meant not letting an assassin erode who I am or put a wedge between me and my God.

Forgiveness did not mean my anger was gone or that I didn't want the murderer severely punished. I would not be human if I retreated from the need to confront evil so that it can be overcome. Justice must be the final chapter in any tragedy, not revenge. We cannot make the mistake of seeing other human beings as worthless, unredeemable, or unloved by God. And therein lies the greatest paradox of all, that God loves both the one who is hurt and the one who has done the hurting. Although this is hard to understand, it is a truth.

That is why the words most often used by Jesus in his ministry were forgiveness and mercy. He acknowledged that these directives are hard to take. He taught us by his words and his life that to follow him—to be a Christian—meant that we had to be different. We had to give up the me-centered life where ego is supreme and take on the true self. We had to undergo the difficult transformation of becoming a clone of the son of God.

Jesus said that being like him meant we would be a contradiction to the world. This is especially true when we embrace his bottom line teaching to overcome evil with good—another way of saying "forgive."

People of forgiveness

There are so many stories of people whose lives are models of forgiveness. I think of what Francis of Assisi said, "Preach the gospel at all times. If necessary, use words." And people who overcome evil with good don't need words to spread the gospel message.

One such person was the late Fr. Lawrence Martin Jenco, a former Beirut hostage who suffered nineteen months of torture and deprivation at the hands of his captors. He called "forgiving and being forgiven...a liberating experience." In an address at a National Conference on Forgiveness held in April of 1995 at the University of Wisconsin in Madison, Fr. Jenco emphasized, "I do not forget the pain, the loneliness, the ache, the terrible injustice...(but) when you can think of the hurt with feelings of gratitude, peace, and even joy, you know you are healed."

His beautiful message has been evident in the action of many people who have forgiven those who hurt them and thus found a sweet freedom. Certainly Pope John Paul II was truly being Christlike when he immediately forgave the man who tried to kill him more than a decade ago. Our Holy Father personally visited his would-be assassin, Mehmet Ali Agca, in Rome's Rebibbia prison after the murder attempt. His forgiveness extended to Agca's whole family. The pontiff even met in a private audience with the mother and brother of this man.

One of the most touching news stories I ever read was how the late Joseph Cardinal Bernardin of Chicago forgave the man who had falsely accused him of having sexually abused him years earlier. I can't imagine how devastatingly painful it must have been for the Cardinal to have been publicly humiliated by this vicious charge. Yet what an example he gave us when he sought a meeting of reconciliation to extend forgiveness to this troubled man, stating that he bore no ill will toward him. More so, Bernardin taught us that this pain had even contributed to his own spiritual growth and made him more compassionate.

When the story of his meeting with his accuser, Steven Cook, who later died from AIDS, was published, the Cardinal's own words were, "May this story of our meeting be a source of joy and grace to all who read it. May God be praised." Bernardin's reconciliation with Cook paralleled what Jesus himself would have done and was a beautiful example of forgiveness.

My own daughter Mary gave me such joy when she was able to say, finally, that she had forgiven her brother Peter for his suicide. Suicide by a family member may be the hardest of all agonies to forgive because it feels so much like a deliberate offense against the parents and siblings, a denial of love for them. I knew this wasn't true in Peter's case.

I had seen the pain Peter suffered from his periodic psychotic breakdowns, so well hidden from others, for nearly eleven years. Sadly, he had fallen into despair and believed he would find peace only by "going home." He had been fond of quoting C.S. Lewis, who wrote that "Earth is not our permanent home." I was never angry at Peter for making his choice to "go home," only devastated. I could forgive him from the beginning. It took his siblings a longer time to be able to say "I forgive him."

In an article for *The Church Herald*, Mary wrote of the process she had to go through in order to forgive Peter:

The night of my baby's christening I sank into bed with a rare feeling of wholeness, basking in the peace and security of what had seemed a perfect day. Sophia's baptism had been shared that morning by family and a loving church community. My brother Peter was my daughter's godfather. But shortly after midnight, as I slept happily, Peter walked to the old swamp in back of my mother's house and put a bullet through his head.

The wake-up call, that news-breaking, heart-ripping telephone call filled me with a pain so excruciating I thought I'd never stand up again. It took about a week after my brother's suicide for anger to set in. It came and went. Sometimes I'd scream curses to the empty air as if the wind would carry my rage to him. How could you do this to us? How could you betray our friendship and trample on my love for you? How could you have tarnished the memory of my baby's christening? How could you be so selfish?

But then my heart moved to Pete's agony. He had suffered acute anxiety for thirteen hellish years. He had served in the military, finished college, taught school at home and abroad, and written three books. He had searched courageously and creatively to find a place in the world, but a pervasive and inexplicable shame followed him everywhere. He despised himself for his failures and for his existence. Therapy had never helped and probably never would have. Peter was too complex, too confused, too passionate, too wounded, and too sensitive. There was no slot on earth into which he could have fit neatly, and he couldn't accept the idea of a life on the fringe of society without a respectable position at its center.

It is very hard for a suicide survivor to believe that anyone's pain could justify that fatal, irreversible act. I myself wouldn't have been able to believe it if I hadn't been so close to suicide myself when I was younger. But I know what helped turn my life around. I had an epiphany experience; from nowhere I felt God freely give me the grace with which I could begin to forgive myself for being alive.

To forgive is just what the word itself says—to offer a gift before it's been earned or even deserved. Pete never had that experience in his heart. He never gave that gift to himself. The least I can do is offer him my forgiveness now because I remember his pain and I love him so much.

Mary was so on target with her definition of "to forgive...." That is how God treats us, and that is why to forgive is so difficult, because it means acting as God would. It doesn't mean to give in; it means to let go. If we don't forgive, we stay emotionally handcuffed to the person or persons that hurt us. And if we are handcuffed we are not free, never at peace, never able to do God's work. Forgiveness is like a boomerang: the gift we send out is what we are going to get back.

There is one other dimension to forgiveness that people of faith must accept and embrace, and that is the sad truth that sin and evil do not affect only the perpetrator. Every act against God is socially destructive; it hurts his entire family. The fallout effect of sin is akin to the feather pillow story the nuns used to tell us. Do you remember it? It goes like this: if you cut a feather pillow and a wind comes along, never again can you collect those scattered feathers.

Sin—be it murder, theft, gossip, sexual license, cheating, or any other way of hurting one another—spreads far and wide. It chains and taints all of us because we are of the same family and come from the same Source. We belong to one another. Fr. Gerald Vann writes of this connectedness, which means we must also face our "solidarity in sin." He says, "Wherever injustice is done in the world, I am involved, I must take a share of the blame; and if I am responsible then I must labor to redress the injustice."

The work that is involved here is nothing less than removing the obstacles and barriers that stand in the way of an intimate union with God, the world, and others. Forgiveness links humanity with divinity, and thus becomes the context whereby we can be reconciled with each other and with the Lord.

In his book, *The Reconciling Community*, James Dallen calls forgiveness

...an essential dimension of Christian spirituality and a condition of spiritual growth." He emphasizes that, "individuals should not be encouraged to reflect on the need for forgiveness simply in terms of personal sins, but rather in terms of their broader responsibilities to community and thus to

God....It is in this way that forgiveness of others is part of spiritual growth.

With forgiveness comes a surprising gift, that is, a sense of freedom and joy. This was confirmed for me by a passage from a book by Louis Evely, called *That Man Is You*. I would like to pass on this wonderful insight.

You see, forgiving kindly entails humbling oneself. The prodigal's father doesn't want to hear another word about the whole episode. He gives a banquet. That's how God does it, too. He alone can make forgiveness something glorious to remember.

CHAPTER SIX

God's "Magic" Surprises

If God directs the course of events at all, then he directs the movement of every atom at every moment; "not one sparrow falls to the ground" without that direction.

▶ C.S. LEWIS

Some years back, I flew to France. During the early morning hours of the flight, the gloriously awakening sun lit up the British Isles as we passed over them. It was light as I had never seen it before, a radiance so brilliant I felt as if I were being blessed and drawn into the glory of the heavens. In that rapturous moment, I knew I had felt God in yet another of his powerful, mysterious ways, and I thanked him through tears of joy.

From this experience it was easy for me to understand the mystics and the saints who experienced extraordinary, intimate, and unearthly revelations of God's love. I learned that these revelations were not just valentines for the saintly. The signs of God's love are all around us, manifested in uncountable ways. Some of these verge on the miraculous but others are subtle, often passed over and unrecognized.

But many people *do* recognize the signs of how God manifests his connection to us and to his creation. Some have written insightfully about these signs. The poet William Wordsworth wrote that we can be gifted or surprised by "a flash of the mystery of the invisible world." And Alfred Lord Tennyson, awed by the God who would let us share his marvelous, mysterious world, wrote: "For I dipped into the future far as human eye could see. Saw the vision of the world and all the wonder that would be."

It was G.K. Chesterton who really excited me. He saw everything in creation—rain, sunshine, clouds, the earth, trees—as radically mysterious in and of themselves, not truly explainable by science. The fact that the moon appears is not because science makes it *necessary*, but because, he maintains, it simply happens. Chesterton writes,

> When we are asked why eggs turn into birds or fruits fall in autumn, we must answer exactly as the fairy godmother would answer if Cinderella asked her why mice turned into horses or her clothes fell from her at twelve o'clock. We must answer that it is magic....A tree grows fruit because it is a magic tree. Water runs downhill because it is bewitched.

He used fairy-tale words like charm, spell, and enchantment to explain the richness of nature, which he saw to be arbitrary and mysterious. In this whimsical mood, clearly marveling at the miraculous and wonderful world, Chesterton goes deeper, noting that all this couldn't have happened by chance. Something or someone must have been behind it all. And so he writes, "In short, I had always believed that the world involved magic; now I thought that perhaps it involved a Magician." In other words, "If there is a story, there must be storyteller." He concludes that the universe may be a mystery for us, but it can't possibly be a mystery for the one who made it.

Chesterton's faith was one I could joyfully share. I think we do live in a magic world, and that we are closely connected to it. Our origins give us a clue. Consider what it says in the Book of Genesis: "...then the Lord God formed man from the dust of the ground, and breathed into his nostrils the breath of life; and the man became a living being" (2:7). When I was a kid it used to bother me that we were made from lowly dust. I used to mumble that God could have made us from starlight or sun rays, from clouds or wind. But, no, it had to be dust. Why?

Perhaps it is because humankind must always know we have a continuity with nature. I believe God made us from the earth so that we would remember we are one with all this glorious magic. Maybe God made us from earth so we could really believe him when he said he would show us, through the resurrection of his son, that we were made for eternal life. Because we are made from earth, we should be able to identify with the ways in which nature hangs on to life and so be able to believe that this is our destiny, too—to be reborn after we die, to live again.

I have studied a lot of science over the years, and I have learned that nothing in nature dies. Everything lives again in one form or another, constantly rebounding from the earth.

One day I walked to the pond where my son Peter had killed himself. To my shock, people had been there and thrown all kinds of garbage and litter on its banks. But then on top of some discarded plastic bags, I found little sprouts of green coming through decaying leaves. I was awed at how nature persists in nurturing life, and brings back beauty even through trash. I took this as a sign from the Lord that he was nurturing Peter in his new life. I was struck by the realization that we breathe because God put his breath in us, as he put breath in all of nature. Because his breath is eternal, resurrection is the great theme of nature. How great is a God who made his creation for eternal life. That is how important we and all of creation are. That is the magic of the Lord.

The power of prayer

God is full of surprises, especially for those who have faith and who pray. In recent years, research has shown that both faith and prayer can have noticeable therapeutic effects. Even scientists and physicians have come to acknowledge this. The power of prayer has been given a prominent place in the writing of Dr. Larry Dossey, who calls himself a proponent of the intimate relationship between physical health and spiritual awareness. His documented research shows that prayer can be a powerful force in healing.

A British surgeon and psychiatrist named Dr. Kenneth McAll gave one of the most memorable witnesses I ever heard on how the power of prayer can result in "spiritual healing." During a lecture at the State University of New York at Stony Brook, he said he had spent the better part of his life "hunting for the spiritual reality of what healing is all about."

McAll had first become interested in spiritual healing in the late 1930s when he became a missionary physician in China. Arrested after the outbreak of World War II, he was put into a Japanese prison camp and remained there four years. His experience as a prisoner of the Japanese was astounding, as he related it in a soft voice and distinctly British accent:

> People in all the camps were in a crude position medically, no medications, not even aspirin or bandages. We were suffering from bronchial diseases, vitamin deficiencies, and the like. Yet, in our camp, people would get better. This was different from the other camps. In those camps, the prisoners were dying. The Japanese were baffled over us....[But] there was only one difference between us and the others: we prayed for one another.

The remarkable phenomenon of what Dr. McAll referred to as the "spontaneous remission of illness" fascinated him. "I saw this happen so many times, related not to doctors or drugs but to prayer and spiritual experiences, that I began seeking to discover what it was about." His quest to understand spiritual healing— which he said he preferred to call "deliverance into new life"— brought the surgeon to conduct a study of why some people get well when others have prayed for them.

Over fifteen years, he recorded some 600 cases where prayer and not medical science was apparently the factor in a person's healing.

He told of case after case where people with phobias, obsessions, schizophrenia, tuberculosis, and other disorders were cured and remained cured after he, along with various clergy and laypeople, had prayed for them. As a result, he had remained deeply Christian and committed to exploring the subject of "taking the problems to the Lord." His work achieved recognition in England and led to his being invited to speak around the world on his convictions about spiritual healing.

Dr. McAll repeated several times that "The physician alleviates and contains—but God heals." This speaks of the essence of faith, affirming that life is all about the relationship between ourselves and God. After hearing him, any skepticism I may have had at that time about the role of faith in healing was defeated, turning to wonder and openness. Who is to say that the hand of God doesn't stretch across the two worlds of spirit and matter? We would be fools to think that we know even a minuscule fraction about the mysteries of creation. As Chesterton said, it involves a Magician and his magic.

My own experience with the therapeutic effects of prayer probably had much to do with why I was so taken by Dr. McAll's affirmation of how God works magic in healing. Back in 1972, I had developed a growth on my thyroid gland. It was a malady that ran in the family. Already my mother and my sister Jeannette had been similarly afflicted, and both had had surgery.

My family doctor sent me to a radiologist who said I needed an operation. I said that I couldn't have one. At the time I was a single parent, supporting and caring for my six children. I couldn't imagine how I could handle being in a hospital and taking the time to recuperate when I had so many responsibilities. And so the doctor decided to try to shrink the growth with a steroid. Truly believing that God would help me, I embarked on a program of prayer. Within two weeks, the tumor unexplainably shrank—disappeared—and to this day, I have never had a recurrence of the problem. I am still on my prayer program, but now everything I say to the Lord is a variation of "thank you."

Sometime later I read an article in *Reader's Digest* called "A

Doctor's Prayer." In it, Dr. William F. Haynes, Jr., told of a patient of great faith being healed, an experience, he wrote, that

...confirmed my determination to call upon the power of prayer. Many doubt such power; I know otherwise. In the lives of my patients and in my own life, I have seen the darkness disappear, the light come back. There is inner peace; miracles can happen; healings do occur; prayers are heard.

We know, of course, that not everyone is physically healed. Each of us can tell a story of someone who wanted to live and prayed for health, but didn't get well. I don't think this means that God ignored the prayer but rather that he had another gift in mind for the sufferer.

My sister Loretta, a physical therapist, has worked with many AIDS patients, mostly young men who are close to death. One day she called me to talk about an AIDS patient who had died. This was a young man she dearly loved, and she was with him at the end. Shortly before he died, the young man had told Loretta that he needed a little boost of faith to help him on his final journey. And so she prayed he would find this boost. When Loretta went back to see the young man later that day, he appeared to be distracted, and so she asked him what was the matter. He looked at her and asked, "Who is this little boy?"

Loretta was confused because there was no little boy in the room. Yet her patient insisted the boy was there, and he wanted to know that Loretta saw him. "I knew then that he was truly seeing a boy and I was sure this was someone sent to him from beyond—maybe his guardian angel—to help him let go," she said. "And so I asked him, 'What does the boy want?'"

"He wants me to take his hand," her patient answered. "Do you trust him?" my sister asked. The young man nodded. "Then why don't you take his hand?" Loretta said, encouraging him. It was as if he needed her assurance that this was what he should do. He smiled. "Yes," he said. He extended his hand, took a long and very peaceful breath, and was on his way. Loretta knew that God answered her prayer in his own loving, magical way.

Our lives are full of God's surprises, sometimes given to us in unusual or humorous ways but always designed to let us know he is near, intimately bound up with our lives. One such incident happened when I was driving home from the grocery store one day. At one point, I had to suddenly slow down because a huge white truck had pulled out of a side street directly in front of me. I was annoyed until I noticed that, printed on the truck in big black letters was 1-800-DIAL GOD. Huh? Was this an omen of some sort, a peculiar joke, or a message I should pay attention to?

I can't say how many times I have wanted to pick up the phone and dial God. I have so many questions for him, beginning with, "Are you a she?" Sometimes I have just wanted to place an order, like, "Could we get rid of the drought (snow, rain, whatever), please?" Sometimes I have just wanted to have a conversation with a loving Father, perhaps asking, "God, could you help me figure out what I should do when I see a beloved friend with lung cancer still smoking?"

Sometimes I have wanted to dial God to demand an explanation for so much tragedy and pain in this world. Sometimes I have wanted to give God a buzz just to chat about the dumb things I see people doing, as well as the cruel and sad things I read about. My question would be, "Considering all the havoc that free will causes, are you sorry for giving it to us? Was it some kind of cosmic mistake?" Sometimes I have wanted to call just to say, "Today I saw the most glorious sunrise, and I want to thank you for giving us so much beauty." Most times I have wanted to dial God to honestly say thanks for the big family I have been blessed with, for all the love I have been given, for the gift of learning, for laughter, for churches, for angels, and even for computers, television, and the telephone.

Well, by this time, the driver in the big white truck had decided to make a right turn. Along the broad side of the vehicle, I saw the invitation again: 1-800-DIAL-GOD. Then, in big letters one or two feet lower, were the words "Guaranteed Overnight Delivery." I had a good laugh at that. What a clever, eye-catching gimmick! That's the American way.

As I continued home that day, it struck me that I have regularly been dialing God through the connection I learned so long ago, the wireless service called prayer. And I have always gotten an answer, either instantly or overnight. It has not always, or even often, been the answer I called for. God's packages are most often gift-wrapped in mystery. Yet I have found each time that what God eventually sent in answer to my call was somehow the right fit. I just had to learn how to read and interpret the directions, confident that this package was delivered in order to help move me along on my faith journey.

Ironically, the unexpected message from black letters on a white truck reminded me that I can get connected to my God any time with prayer—and that has always been faster than a phone call.

The hand of God

Anne Manduca had an incident similar to mine, involving a truck that suddenly appeared while she was driving. After reading my book, *Coincidences: Touched by a Miracle*, she wrote to tell me her own "miracle" story.

Anne had been married for thirty-seven years to a man who did all the driving. When he decided to end the marriage, Anne had to learn to be on her own. One night, returning home from a relative's birthday party in Brooklyn, she missed the turn she needed to take to get on the road to her home out on Long Island. "In an attempt to return to a point that was familiar to me, I got even further into an area that was uncharted territory," she wrote, adding that she started crying out to God to help her. Anne continued,

Within one minute, the front part of a white tractor trailer pulled up next to me. The wheel flaps read, "Transportation for Christ." I couldn't believe my eyes. I followed the truck for about four minutes into an area that you would warn your kids not to drive through alone. The driver parked the truck, and I asked him for help. He said yes, and led me to an entry for the Long Island Expressway. As we approached the ramp I needed to take, he pulled over. Out came my angel. He stopped traffic so I could make a left onto the ramp from the right lane. I yelled "God bless you, thank you," and headed home, knowing I was just touched by the hand of God.

I hear so many stories that convince me God is always handing out "magic" surprises. Paul Jackson wrote to tell me he was traveling with his wife and daughter when they got sidetracked. It was a Saturday and they were lucky to find a hotel, but just as important to them was the need to find a Catholic church that had a Saturday night Mass because they had to be on their way very early the next morning. The hotel clerk told them they were out of luck, but added that his parish church, a distance away, had a Sunday morning Mass. Jackson decided it would be wise to check out the church's location to make sure they would get there on time in the morning. He writes,

We followed directions, found the church....Our daughter went in, found a bulletin, came running out waving it, saying, "Dad, you're not going to believe this, but they're having a special Mass in Latin at 8:00 PM. tonight, with the North Atlanta Chorus and Symphonic Orchestra singing and playing," We went and it was a beautiful Eucharistic feast, with great music and song.

It was not by accident that this family got to Mass that night. "What a gift of the Spirit to put the idea into my head that we should check out the church," was the way Mr. Jackson and his family saw it—just another tale of the surprising, and sometimes humble way, God stays in touch.

Jesus said that if we believe in him, he would be with us always. I have often had moments in my life when Jesus is exceptionally present and I would wager that this often happens to people of faith. For example, I shall never forget an incident that occurred on Christmas morning of 1992. I was in the kitchen beginning to prepare food for the dinner I was making for my big family. My son-in-law Rick was the only other person up that early. He decided to set up the fireplace, stacking the wood so that later, when everyone was ready to open gifts, we could have a nice, quickly starting fire.

When Rick had finished, he stood in the doorway between the family room and the kitchen, and we began talking about religion. I told Rick that I had spent many years reading books on various religions, spirituality, mythology, mysticism and so on, emphasizing "But what I have learned in doing this is that all the wisdom I ever need I find in the words of Jesus."

At that moment, Rick let out a "wow!" I turned to look at him and asked, "What's the matter?" "Come quick," he said. I walked over to where he was standing and saw that the fireplace was ablaze, like a burning bush. Rick told me that as I made my declaration of faith in Jesus, the wood in the fireplace had burst into flame. The fireplace was cold. He had not lit a match. We stood for a moment in disbelief, trying to explain scientifically something that had no scientific explanation, as Chesterton would have commented.

Rick and I both felt we had been given a gift that Christmas morning, that the Lord had given us the sign of the "burning bush" as a Christmas gift, his approving response to my affirmation of faith in him.

While God's "magic" is all around us, it is most powerfully manifested in the way certain people touch us, becoming visible signs of his love by the faith that radiates from them. Janet Schmidt was one of these special people. About two years ago, Janet, whom I didn't know then, called me out of the blue. She had read my book *Coincidences*, and noting that we lived in the same town, wanted to meet me. She asked if I was interested in hearing about the coincidences that had led her to become a Catholic. I told her to come over right away.

A week or so earlier, I had been in my son Paul's gallery in New York—he deals in coins and medals—and had bought a lovely medal of Thérèse of Lisieux from him. I felt that someone was going to come along who would be just right for that beautiful silver medal. I put it on the table for Janet.

From the moment Janet entered my house and saw that medal, the surprises started. With a joyous tear, she told me that it was

Thérèse who had led her to the Church! Her story began back in July of 1996, when, having survived breast cancer, she was diagnosed with a metasticized recurrence of breast cancer. Janet said, "A Catholic friend who was married to a Jewish man, while I was Jewish married to a Catholic, joyfully told me she had said a novena to Thérèse for my healing. She told me Thérèse is called the 'Little Flower' and is always pictured with roses."

To Janet's surprise, someone gave her a silk rose on her birthday, and she took the unexpected rose as a sign that God was listening to her friend's prayer. Later, her friend told her not to be surprised if more roses came her way. Janet had just arrived home from visiting with her friend when her cleaning lady showed up with two dozen roses. Then "the messages," myriad roses from Thérèse, began in earnest.

A powerful message came when Janet was in New York getting treatment at the famed cancer hospital, Memorial Sloan-Kettering. She felt a strong pull to go to St. Patrick's Cathedral, so her husband, Stephen, took her. There she felt "a miracle happening. The entire church was filled with something about Thérèse. It was the centennial of her death. I was so overwhelmed." There was a table with books, and on it she saw one called *How to Pray with St. Thérèse of Lisieux*, written by an author named, like herself, Schmidt. "It was like a brick hitting me over the head," said Janet.

Even as her cancer escalated, the incredible appearances of roses kept assuring Janet that Thérèse was with her. When she asked her husband's pastor, Fr. Al Audette, what it would take to be baptized, he asked in his typical good humor, "Got water?"

Sadly, Janet's cancer won out and she died in September of 1999. During the beautiful funeral service led by Fr. Al, I prayed to Thérèse to let me see an unexpected rose as a sign that she was taking care of Janet. When I got home, I walked around my house and suddenly saw, sprouting from an old rose bush that hadn't bloomed in two years, a glorious huge red rose! Through tears of joy, I thanked Thérèse for her instant answer to my prayer, and I thanked God for having such a great crew of saints to help him spread his "magic" around.

The world abounds with remarkable stories and people love to hear them. Sales of inspirational books, particularly those telling stories of angels and miracles, have been brisk in recent years. Magazines, too, contain tales of angels coming to the rescue of people in trouble. I enjoy reading these stories, but this overemphasis on wanting to hear about spectacular miracles worries me a bit.

A few years back, the author of one of the earliest and best-known angel books gave a talk in Connecticut, drawing in a crowd of hundreds. The next day, I received a call from a woman I know, who is, like myself, the mother of a son who committed suicide. This woman was not happy. She had gone to the talk and heard about many profound miracles. But all this did for her was generate intense pain as the question kept tormenting her: "Where were the angels when my son needed them?"

From her perspective, God is simply too selective when it comes to dispensing the big miracles, the capital letter type miracles that make it into the angel books. This may be true. We will never really find out why miracles sometimes occur, why, for example, some people are spontaneously healed from a terminal illness. What we do know is grand miracles require that God change the laws he put into place for running this universe. But it is not God's plan to change the universe, and that is why there are so few miracles of this kind. Even for saintly people proposed for canonization, the miracle gap looms large. The Church requires authenticated miracles to have occurred through their intercession, and sometimes decades and centuries go by before proven miracles happen.

Small "m" miracles

I believe in miracles, but the spectacular ones are like frosting on the cake. From our human perspective, we may grumble that there is an element of unfairness about who gets one of the "big ones" and who doesn't. But we don't have all the data, and so we are only speaking from our ignorance when we try to get into God's mind. All we know is that miracles with a big "M" are scarce. As C.S. Lewis said, "God does not shake miracles into Nature at random as if from a pepper-caster." What God does is give us equally won-derful miracles, the small "m" kind. If we open our eyes and our hearts, we can see and feel these miracles all around us. And some-times we just call them coincidences.

Could this incident, sent to me by Paul Waldman, who long worked for *Liguorian* magazine, be anything less than a miracle? Paul told of how a sudden snowstorm had come up one day while he was at home with his wife, Florence. They were practically out of food, so they drove to the supermarket, loaded two carts with food, paid the bill, and walked out. By this time, the parking lot was a sheet of ice. Florence, holding on to her cart, began slipping on the ice. Paul said he was desperate for help.

Suddenly a young man in a military-type jacket came up to us, took my cart, and pulled it toward my car without asking which my car was. At the same time, another young man, dressed the same way and with the same features, came up to Florence and told her, "Hold on to my arm." I followed the first young man, who at that point asked, "Which is your car?" I told him and he repeated, "the blue Buick."

Paul thanked the men, saying he could put the bags of food into the car without help. The two walked away without a word. Were they angels sent from God? Or were they just two well-raised, kind young men who happened to be in the parking lot at the same time as the Waldmans? What difference does it make? What they did was God in action, a miracle, not the kind that would qualify anyone for canonization, but a magic God-moment nonetheless.

I constantly hear faith-affirming stories like this. Consider the danger a twenty-three-year-old tractor trailer driver was in on a November day in Ohio. He was hauling turkeys, and had bent down to pick something up when he lost control of his vehicle and hit the guardrail. This ripped open the truck's fuel lines and engulfed the truck in flames. Two truckers stopped to try to free the driver from the wreckage, but the heat of the flames forced them back.

What happened next is amazing. A third trucker stopped. He picked up a fire extinguisher, smashed open a sun-roof window above the cab's sleeping compartment, and pulled the young driver out. The rescuer was in his truck and heading away before anyone found out who he was, according to witnesses.

Who was he? An angel? Just a smart-thinking truck driver? Was this a miracle? Of course it was, only with a small "m." This was still more proof that a Benevolent Force is in this world, a loving parent who cares so much for each of us that he even counts the hairs on our heads.

For anyone who has ever felt this Force, the experience remains ever-vibrant. Lloyd Faulkner of Oklahoma sent me a letter telling me of an experience he had on Christmas Day back in 1932, when he was six years old.

> Mom and Dad went to town on an errand. While they were gone, it was my plan to decorate the house, making it cheerful when my parents returned. I was lighting a candle for one of the decorations when my shirt caught afire. I panicked and raced for the front door. Just after leaving the kitchen and on entering the dining room on my way back to the front door, I felt a hand shove me in the middle of my back between my shoulder blades. I was pushed to the carpeted floor, extinguishing the fire. I suffered a rather extensive third-degree burn to my right chest, but I was alive!
>
> I can feel that hand in the middle of my back to this day, so many years later. The good Lord or my guardian angel was with me on that fateful day. Never let anyone say that we can't experience the Divine intervening in our lives, connecting the physical with the spiritual in his love for us.

Gilbert Ortiz of Wyoming is another man who experienced God's magic. It had to do with his getting a letter from the late Mother Teresa—in response to one he had sent her seventeen years earlier! The letter arrived on the same day Mr. Ortiz learned that he had failing kidneys and an aneurysm on his aorta. It came along with another letter from Sister Nirmala Joshi, the superior of the Missionaries of Charity in New York, who wrote that Mother Teresa's letter to Ortiz had just been found at the order's motherhouse. He said,

When I read the letter, I hit the roof. Maybe I hit heaven. In the letter, Mother Teresa told me: "Pain, sorrow, suffering is but the kiss of Jesus. A sign that you have come so close to him that he can kiss you. May God give you all the courage to accept your cross with resignation and love in union with the passion of Jesus. God bless you."

Receiving Mother Teresa's letter on the same day he was given news of his very serious illnesses was a tremendous faith boost for Ortiz. He said that the letter made him "ready to go. Now I know I've got somebody praying for me."

I have folders full of stories like the ones told here that give evidence of how God enchants us and his world with magic. I love the story sent to me by Barbara Bachand:

> I went outside to put something on a short line to dry. As I lifted my hands to the line, I could feel myself being raised up and being held in a huge palm. I felt no fear, only incredible peace. I have no idea how long this occurred. I just basked in the loving peace.
>
> Now when I look back, I'm reminded of the fact that sometimes to pray is to sit and let God love you. When I was lowered to the ground, the leaves that were moving gently on the forsythia bushes gave me a message that I am part of every living thing.

Moments of such intense grace have happened to many people, sometimes in an even more spectacular way. One hundred years ago, in a book called *Cosmic Consciousness*, Dr. Richard Maurice Bucke, a psychiatrist, delved into the lives of many well-known people in history—the apostle Paul, Walt Whitman, Dante, William Blake, Socrates, and William Wordsworth, to name a few—that he judged to have had illuminating mystical experiences. In every instance, these people were surrounded by intense, unearthly light, and felt an indescribable feeling of elevation, elation, joy, a quickened moral sense, and a consciousness of the cosmos, that is, the life and order of the universe. "With these come what may be called a sense of immortality, a consciousness of eternal life, not a conviction that he shall have this, but the consciousness that he has it already," Dr. Bucke affirmed.

One of the men he writes about is John Ypes, better known as John of the Cross. Bucke quotes a biographer of this great saint, who tells of a phenomenon of light that appeared as the saint was escaping from imprisonment in a monastery: "He saw a wonderful light, out of which came a voice, 'Follow me.' He followed and the light moved before him towards the wall which was on the bank, and then he knew not how, he found himself on the summit of it without effort or fatigue."

John of the Cross himself wrote:

> All I say falls short of that which passes in this intimate union of the soul with God....I knew not where I entered, for when I stood within, not knowing where I was, I heard great things. What I heard I will not tell....I stood enraptured in ecstasy....My spirit was endowed with understanding, understanding naught...a sense profound of the essence of God.

While we ourselves may not have had an experience of such profound dimensions, we do have the witness of people who have vividly felt God's presence. Through them, we, too, touch God.

God's ways are baffling and mysterious, yet wondrous. He knocks on the door of our hearts, a door which can only be opened from the inside. When we let him in, the magic starts. A quote attributed to Canon John Andrew, once rector of St. Thomas Episcopal Church in New York, underscores that we are in charge of the doorway to God: "To them, as to all who complain that God has somehow removed himself from their ability to reach him, I am always tempted to ask, 'Who moved?'"

CHAPTER SEVEN

Life's Tough Courses

**The beginning of faith is the beginning of our grop-
ing for understanding—without assuming in advance
that we know the answer.**

▶ WILL OURSLER

I look back at my life and my faith—how I have struggled with it,
how it has confused me, supported me, comforted me, and defined
me—and know, with clarity, that the process is not finished. My
faith has been evolving since I came to the age of reason and continues to do so both in the experiences I personally encounter, and
in those I hear about from others.

I do recall a time, however, when faith was not at all a struggle,
when I was nine and preparing to receive the sacrament of confirmation. Back then we had been taught some interesting things
about this sacrament, most of which just couldn't be translated
into everyday living. This was especially true for girls. By being confirmed, we were told that even little girls became "soldiers of
Christ" and members of his "army." The imagery was totally masculine and hopelessly out of step with the Mary-like virtues girls
were expected to adopt back then.

On the other hand, being considered soldiers of Christ gave us an "in" to the mysterious masculine world. I remember battling bravely, if only verbally, with a fellow fourth-grader during confirmation instructions, insisting that no male would be a better soldier than I when it came to defending the faith. Bravely and gladly would I face martyrdom for Christ, I said in my innocence and ignorance.

I looked forward to the slap the Bishop would give me because, as Sister explained to us, it was a sign of our willingness to suffer in witness of Christ. We were well-prepared. We could recite the catechism, vow fidelity to Christ under pain of death, proudly accept our new role as Christ's soldiers, and affirm that the Holy Spirit had now made us strong and perfect Christians. The truth is that, in reality, we didn't have the foggiest notion of what all this meant.

Following the Second Vatican Council, confirmation got a new package. The military language went out as did the emphasis on glorious martyrdom. Confirmation was now recognized as the sacrament of maturity, of adulthood, not conferred on children after proper preparation but one chosen by youthful, emerging adults making a decision about their life, saying, in effect: "I, Antoinette, fully understanding the love, sacrifice, joys, and crosses intrinsic in living the Christian life, do consciously and freely choose now to follow Christ daily until death, so that through me, Christ is still alive and well and living on this earth."

Although this type of language is a vast improvement over the old language of the sacrament, it can be just as foggy to understand as the promise spoken in the past. What this essentially means is that confirmation cannot be understood simply by talking about it because it is a way of life. With baptism, we are initiated into the life of Christ. Confirmation continues this process. It challenges us to take on Christ's life, the life of faith. It asks us to act as Christ would in all matters so that eventually, being a Christian is so much a part of our nature that to act otherwise would be out of character and altogether wrong. This is parallel to the way a mature person consistently acts like an adult, and does not revert back to childish tantrums, outlandish selfishness, unrelenting stubbornness, a demand for immediate gratification, and other forms of behavior which earmark immaturity.

A person does not become mature, however, simply because he or she has become an adult. One has to work at gaining and maintaining maturity, just as one has to work at taking on the evolutionary task of growing as a Christian today, tomorrow, and the day after. Consider what maturity means: dependability, the acceptance of responsibility, the ability to cope with setbacks, the awareness of one's strong points and admittance of one's limitations. Maturity is characterized by order, good intentions carried out in action, and above all, a permeating courage to support one's determination not to slip backwards and betray one's adulthood by immature actions.

Isn't it obvious how these characteristics of maturity apply to the Christian life? When confirmation is called the sacrament of maturity it underscores the fact that the qualities of maturity are essential to living the Christian life. We are to become clones of Christ, reshaping the world according to Jesus' model of love, justice, peace, joy, and goodness.

There is a story that came out of World War II which tells of a soldier who went back into a small French village that had been bombed and vacated. To his surprise, he found a statue of Christ still standing before the demolished church. The only damage was that the hands of Christ were missing. Then he looked down and saw that someone had made a sign and propped it at the feet of the statue. It read, "I have no hands but yours."

As I meditate on that story, I begin to understand the challenge of carrying on Christ's work to make this world a planet of love. Long ago, I had affirmed that my confirmation meant I was beginning a journey where I would always say "yes" to the Christ of the broken hands and never change my mind, no matter how much the world crushed me with its pain, imperfections, and silence.

To keep this promise has been the greatest challenge, torment, and yet, joy of my life. Since the day of my confirmation at age nine, my faith has been tampered with in day-to-day struggles, faltering when I so often felt abandoned by my silent God. But my faith would always be renewed and strengthened in unexpected ways, through a person I met, a revelation, a personal experience, a book, a movie, and often, through prayer.

The language of God

We have all heard the comment that "God always answers prayers. He says 'yes,' 'no,' or 'you've got to be kidding!'" I smile at that one, but I have learned something else: there is an in-between. Sometimes God answers prayers in a way that is hard to recognize immediately. I also think we have to give God credit for the unique language he often uses in answering prayers.

Here is a case in point. I was scheduled to do a morning interview on a radio station in New York City about my book, *The Pummeled Heart: Finding Peace Through Pain*. I went to New York the night before the interview and stayed with my daughter Mary and her family, who live in Manhattan. The East Coast was experiencing a frigid cold wave at the time, so I decided to allow myself extra time in the morning to get to the interview. I figured that because of the extreme cold, more people than usual would be taking cabs and I might have to wait longer to get a free one.

I was right. I tried hailing a cab for nearly forty minutes before I began to concede that I might not get one. So I started to pray. I asked the Lord to please not let me be late for this important appointment. I asked him to please help me get a cab so I could get to the station and not lose the interview.

Meanwhile, I had walked over to 6th Avenue, figuring this might help me get a cab since the radio station was located at 6th Avenue and 52nd Street, a straight run uptown. But another ten minutes went by, and no cab. God didn't seem to be listening to my prayer, but hey? Who am I to get annoyed at God?

I hadn't noticed that I was at a bus stop, and suddenly, there was a bus. I asked the driver, "Does this go to 52nd Street?" He said yes. I got on, and then saw the sign that said, "exact change only." Coincidentally, I had also visited my son Frank and his family the night before because they too live in New York. When I left to go to my daughter's apartment, he put six quarters into my coat pocket, the fare for a bus, suggesting that at this late hour a bus might come before a cab. Well, I had gotten a cab after all, and so the bus fare was still in my pocket.

I arrived at the radio station by 9:30 AM, exactly when taping was scheduled to begin. Everyone was lovely to me and very understanding about my delay. The taping went well, and I left. I began to pray again, and was about to tell the Lord that I had made my appointment, no thanks to him, when I stopped short. My brain took over and reminded me that what I had really asked for was that I would not be late for the interview, that I could keep my appointment. It struck me then that, of course, the Lord had answered my prayer, not in the specific way I asked for but via his own agenda.

We sometimes expect God to respond to us according to our specifications, serving our every request. And that was exactly how I had acted. I wanted a cab. But God arranged for a bus and six quarters. It just took me a while to understand his language.

The nuns used to tell us to "pray as if everything depended on God, but work as if everything depended on you." Maybe that was part of the lesson I needed to learn that day. God expects us to work things out. He is there to help, but not to sprinkle miracles at our command. My experience that morning had given my faith a boost with the simple revelation that my prayers were answered in God's own way, in his mysterious, loving language.

One could say this was a rather simplistic faith-boosting experience, and I wouldn't argue that. I would only say this: isn't it a good God who helps us get insights about his love and care from even the most ordinary, everyday experiences—not just from those that are extreme, comforting, or traumatic?

I have often gotten a faith-boost by talking to my sister Loretta, a physical therapist. Her hands channel not just love but also her faith, which draws her to the vocation of helping to ease the pain of others. Yet Loretta tells me she gets more than she gives, for she has learned what faith really means from the people she cares for.

One of these patients was an ailing, poor black woman who never complained about anything, even though she had had a very tough life. Loretta told me that the woman looked at her life as a complete blessing: no matter how hard she worked, how much prejudice she was subjected to, how much loss she endured, never did this make her doubt God's love for her. Loretta was so touched by this woman's ability to overlook her troubles and concentrate on the good that she asked her to share her definition of faith. Her patient replied, "Honey, faith means if you pray for rain, bring an umbrella! And honey, if you pray for sun, wear sunglasses!"

What a wonderful relationship to have with the Lord! This woman asked for God's help to get her through the tough, dark places her life had led her, and she believed that this help would come pouring down. She didn't ask for "things"; she asked for endurance, for a sense of always being in the light of her Lord even though she was too poor to get an education, too black to get a break, too female to get ahead, and too wounded to walk. And when she prayed for God's love to rain down on her, she expected a deluge. She bought an umbrella and carried it upside down to catch the downpour of his reassuring "yes." When she asked him to warm her with his sun, she put on the sunglasses in anticipation of how brightly he would light up her life.

I have never stopped thinking about this woman and her marvelous confidence in the Lord. Her trust in God was surely a sign of a faith that evolved from words to a true acceptance of his love—no questions asked. Her believing became her seeing.

Listening to God

As I get older I find myself marveling at all the ways the Lord leads us to believe in him. He has built continuing clues about his presence into this great world of ours, and yearns only that we find them.

The writer Clare Boothe Luce was a convert to Catholicism who saw faith as the essential journey, continually evolving because it is a life-force. She wrote that each individual life is "a seeding time of God, the preparation of that soul for the blossoming of faith," and maintained that God has not let a day go by "without sending someone or something to seek entry for him." Luce affirmed that everything that ever happens to a person "has a supernatural as well as a natural meaning."

I think back on some of the experiences of my life and know that this is absolutely true, though most often the revelation came unexpectedly and after the fact. One such night brought me an insight about God that has remained with me ever since. It happened at a talk given in 1966 by Erich Fromm, the widely respected philosopher and psychoanalyst. At the time, great concern had been raised over a new, brash concept coming out of the writings of a Protestant theologian, Thomas Altizer, who claimed "God is dead." This profane expression had triggered all sorts of reactions from clergy to university professors to ordinary people on the street, whose cars sported bumper stickers saying, "Maybe your God is dead, but mine isn't."

Fromm had accepted an invitation to debate this issue with a Catholic professor at Queens College in New York, and I couldn't stay away. And so I set out from my home some fifty miles away, with my son Paul, then sixteen, along for the ride.

In his remarks, Fromm said that the problem was not at all whether God is dead. As he saw it, the real problem was whether or not man is dead or in danger of dying. If man is dead, he is not there to praise God any more. If man is dead, then God is dead because "God is a living God for living men."

Sadly, Fromm pointed out, man is in danger of dying. He felt that people were deeply unhappy in spite of their mad attempts to make merry by eating, drinking, and otherwise "doping" themselves. What is repressed, he said, is the "underlying anxiety, depression, loneliness, boredom, and pain about the meaninglessness of life." Man attempts to find satisfaction in "fake reality," but by doing so, throws away values and ideals, leaving only the destiny of alienation, which is death.

Fromm's scenario went like this: when humankind produces things and then begins to worship the work of its own hands, we become idolaters. Idols make us powerless. Idolatry puts the idols—things—in control, dominating us. Idols are dead things. But God is living. The central sin, then, is idolatry, human beings worshipping the work of our own hands, a condition that reduces us to nothing more than producers of things.

From there he went on to talk about the gods we worship. He named some: success, material possessions, comfort, sex, education, money, and health. These "gods" dominate us, even though love, reason, justice, maturity, humor, happiness, joy, and serenity should be the earmarks of humankind. When these values are not priorities for living people, then we give to Caesar what is God's.

Fromm did not call for a renewal of specific religions. He was pointing out how secularism—which ignores, denies, and even kills God—becomes the villain, destroying the spirit of man.

Given his background, I was surprised that night to hear Fromm talk so much about God. He had been a practicing, religious Jew until he was twenty-seven years old, but then had became a secular humanist. And now he was asking honestly: how can man, who is dying because he is breaking the fundamental command not to worship idols, be brought back to life? This can only be done, he said, if everyone—religious people and atheists—takes a fresh approach in the common defense of man's soul and sees, really sees, the human realities that are in danger of being lost.

Overwhelmed by the clarity and wisdom presented by this great man, who died in March of 1980, I realized that Fromm's message was neither new nor mysterious to the Christian. It had been lived in the person of Jesus and expressed in his fundamental teachings. Yet Fromm had spoken a truth that shed new light on the ways we kill God. That night, I prayed to internalize his message so my faith could expand. This was only one of a lifetime full of encounters where, as Clare Boothe Luce expressed it, God had acted by "sending someone or something to seek entry for him."

God chooses so many creative ways to get our attention. He especially manages to zero in on our weak points to test whether we can turn these around and find him. He has done this to me many times. I have found one of the hardest tests to be when he makes me wait.

Year ago I was stuck on a train. Up ahead a track was broken and under repair, so we all had to sit in our seats and wait: there was no other choice. I finished reading the book I had brought with me, then sat silently fuming, thinking about all the times we are trapped in the immobile position of waiting. We have all waited in doctors' offices or motor vehicle lines or at checkout counters in the supermarket. People also can wait for hours on end in an unemployment office or at a welfare department or in traffic court. Parents wait for teenage children to come home from a movie or a dance, so preoccupied with their child's absence that no activity can squeeze out the reality of waiting. Prisoners wait for their sentences to end. Sick people wait to be healed.

With nothing to read on the train that day, I began to think about the different ways people react to waiting. Some are patient and can handle the feeling of time standing still. Some are nervous, and twirl their thumbs or pace the floor. Some become angry at time lost. Yet waiting remains one of those conditions which periodically affects every person. It is built into life. Witness how we wait for rain to end, for the sun to shine, for winter to go away and summer to begin. We wait for babies to be born and final illness to end.

If everyone made a list of the things we most disliked, I would suspect that waiting might be on nearly every list. It sure would be on mine! Waiting denotes inactivity and therefore, a lack of productivity. In our world, productivity is considered a primary value, and so any condition which prevents it is usually unwanted. That may include being handicapped, unemployed, retired, in prison, and the like, all types of unproductive conditions.

As these observations went through my mind, I thought of a line from Milton, "They also serve who only stand and wait." For the life of me, I couldn't understand what he meant. I could admit, though, that this line has traveled down through the centuries and is well remembered if only because people identify with it in some way. Could it be that waiting has a useful purpose, that it is not simply a chunk of life lost?

Now I started to go deeper. Maybe life imposes waiting on us so that now and then, we are forced not to do but simply to be. Another poet wrote, "But what is life if, full of care, we have no time to stop and stare?" Maybe waiting is built into existence to remind us that existence itself has value, that we don't need to be productive to be worthwhile. Maybe God is the one behind all this waiting, and arranges to have us stopped in our tracks once in a while so we can "stop and stare." If we don't, imagine how much of his beautiful world we are going to miss.

The train eventually got going, but in the meantime I had learned that God is behind all of our waiting. Sometimes waiting may be the only way he can get us to serve him, instead of our jobs or whatever. It may be the way God invites us to stop and stare so we can rediscover the wonder of his world and our importance as his offspring. Ralph Waldo Emerson wrote, "The whole course of things goes to teach us faith," and that includes the experience of waiting.

While I can find something every day that sparks my faith, in all honesty I must also admit that I struggle daily not to fall into disbelief. When you lose children, you live in permanent pain and can experience recurrent bouts of anger at what life has brought. Sometimes the anger gets pointed at God, not to blame him for the deaths but for the fact that we have to die at all. I wonder if Jesus himself felt that anger.

I can imagine that when Jesus, who was just a carpenter's son to his peers, began preaching and creating an outrageous stir, he was wise enough to know he would make enemies. He had to know that as he faced pain and death he would lose the brightness of the noonday sun and his mission would become fuzzy in the ensuing gloom. At the end of his earthly life, he fell into a pit when he felt betrayed and abandoned by the Father.

Out of a need not to capitulate to darkness, Jesus retreated to the desert to wrestle with his doubts, to recharge his beliefs and energies, to solidify his determination to see his difficult mission through and not waiver, come betrayal and cross, from his mission: "For this was I born." Jesus spent forty days being besieged by the deceiver. But he kept the faith, building up his trust in the Father and gaining the courage to face what was to come, not knowing for sure if there was a light at the end of the tunnel, a road at the end of the forest, an Easter after the execution.

I have been there with Jesus, plagued with the vagaries of a faith which could be as comforting as a warm blanket one minute and as tormenting as a fickle lover the next. What consoled me throughout was that I could retreat with him to the desert. There I too could listen to the Father, rediscover trust in his love, and reaffirm fidelity to him so as not to break down in the blackness of the cross.

This uneasy faith is our heritage because it is subject to all the ups and downs of life itself. When all is well and life is pleasant, faith is an easy part of the package. But life also brings the death of a child, the divorce of parents, a grown child turned selfish and ugly, a debilitating illness, a desperate boredom, an untouchable loneliness, or confinement to an old age home. How many of us are so strong in our faith that we can face these terrifying conditions with the clarity of knowing that God is still with us?

I am always walking a tightrope between the "yes" and "no" of my faith. But I haven't fallen off yet because of Jesus. I go back with him for those forty days of searching, scared stiff about the crosses lying in wait for me yet gaining courage from the remembrance that Jesus himself wasn't spared the cross. If he could go on to face Good Friday not knowing with certainty that there would be an Easter Sunday—remember his cry, "Father, why have you forsaken me?"—can't I hang in there, too? Can't I go on believing that no matter where I stand in the darkness, there is a hand there to lead me to the light?

The answers to my questions lie in Jesus. Louis Evely, the noted French spiritual writer, expressed his faith in these words: "I give thanks to Jesus Christ for having revealed to me the human countenance of God and that Power of love which is stronger than all evil." I second that.

CHAPTER EIGHT

Faith Is Alive in Deeds

Have you not noticed that as a man ceases to believe in God, he also ceases to believe in man? You could not point to a single person who truly loves God and is mean to his fellow man. ▶ BISHOP FULTON J. SHEEN

I once read a book with a title that really grabbed me: *How Can I Find God?* The author, James Martin, a Jesuit scholastic preparing for ordination, wrote the book after a close friend who had lost touch with religion and church asked him that question. After responding as best he could, Martin decided to ask people of many different faiths how they would answer her question.

I couldn't count the times I have been asked that same question, especially in the past decade when I have worked with so many people who are grieving and hurting. The question comes from the depths of their souls, and I hear in it a deep mourning which comes from the sense of being lost. And so I share what I have learned, that while faith may seem dead in these dark times, it is not; it is only dormant.

Faith can come alive again, sometimes suddenly, by the simple, caring touch of another person. Faith is alive not because we speak words, but because we see God in all that surrounds us, in every person ever born. Our faith is alive when we act as Jesus would. As Louis Austin, a West Virginia innkeeper and very spiritual man, put it, "Our Maker gave us two hands. One to hold to him; the other to extend to our fellow man."

Martin's book contains reflections from sixty-eight people, some famous, some unknown, on the question "how can I find God?" In reading the book, I sense that most of the people who responded stumbled a bit before organizing their thoughts enough to put them down on paper. After all, this question goes to the heart of everything about us, from our origins to our destiny, and it is never easy to put something that profound into words. But there was certainly a common theme in the responses: that is, we can't think about God without moving into the realm of love and relationship with others.

Dr. Robert Coles, the famed Harvard child psychiatrist and writer, answered directly:

> We find God, I think, through others—through the love we learn to offer them, through the love we learn to receive from them—no small achievement and indeed a lifelong effort. We find God with difficulty—the obstacle of pride is always there.

The briefest answer came from Holocaust survivor and Nobel Peace Prize winner Elie Wiesel. "How do I find God? you ask. I do not know how, but I do know where—in my fellow man."

"First of all, relax, and be assured that God is also seeking you," points out Kathleen Norris, poet and author of the books *Dakota: A Spiritual Geography* and *The Cloister Walk*.

Chris Erikson, a thirty-three-year-old Nebraska farmer, responds with visionary, muted passion:

> How can we find God? He is all around us. The essence of our very existence. When we look at God's creation, we see the wonderful work of the Almighty Hand. I find God in the

soil I till, the crops I grow, the water I use—all working together to provide food....I see God in other people through their acts of kindness and caring. And I believe you can find God in the way our universe functions, in the intricate and magnificent way it operates....If you have faith, all you have to do is open your eyes and God is easy to find.

I can imagine many people saying "I agree" to the very things quoted here, for they are good, wise, and true. But yet, another observation haunts me: why is it that some people believe they are good and reach out to others with love, empathy, and understanding, yet act in a way that is most unlovable? If there is a difference between what we say and how we act, faith becomes stagnant.

I was in the third grade when this truth first struck home. We had been given a poem to read in class, about a family of young children who claimed to love their mother. Each line in the poem started out with one of the children saying, "I love you, Mother...." Then the child would go out to play or do something else strictly in his or her own interest. The last coupling was different.

"I love you, Mother," said little Nan.
"Today I'll help you all I can."

The poem then went on to ask, which one of the children do you think loved their mother best? This poem unlocked an awareness in me at a very early age that the mouth can be like "a noisy gong or a clanging cymbal," to use a well-known phrase from St. Paul (1 Cor 13), if the words it generates aren't orchestrated in action.

Faith in action

In every aspect of life, we communicate more truly by what we do than by what we say. This is especially true for faith. A classic example of this happened on a Sunday afternoon back in the 1960s. I was marching with about twenty friends and our young children, most of us from our Diocesan Catholic Interracial Council. We were protesting the refusal of the local all-volunteer fire department to let a black man, who was a respected community member, join the fire department.

As we marched back and forth in front of the firehouse, carrying signs that read "equality," the firemen began to drive the fire trucks out the doors. They parked the trucks between us and the building, and began to wash them. Naturally, most of the water fell on us. It was frightening for the children, who all started screaming in fear. Over the roar of rushing water, the firemen, a majority of them Catholic, laughed loudly, apologized, and said that our getting drenched was an "unfortunate accident." Ironically, most of these men had just attended Mass together, then gone to their annual Communion breakfast.

I have often wondered if any of these men, who earlier that day had received Holy Communion as a body, even considered what they did in drenching us to be a matter of conscience and faith. And what about the issue of prejudice? Where did that fit in with their faith?

In families, deeds that make a mockery of faith occur on a smaller scale, but their effect can be magnified by proximity. In a family, words can't patch up reality. To claim "I love you," while husbands, wives, and children assault one another in a variety of ways, is the worst of lies, casting faith into jeopardy.

For decades now the expression "body language" has been commonly used to describe the way every gesture, motion, expression, and even breath communicates what we really feel. The concept of body language acknowledges how clearly we speak without words, and how empty words can be if not backed up with substance.

Many years after I had first read that poem in third grade, I came upon another poem which hit a chord with me. It delivered the same message as the poem I had heard early on, but I now heard the message on a more mature level, a level in keeping with my age and developed sense of Christian responsibility. I have kept it in a special folder so as to never forget its challenge of words versus deeds. I don't know who wrote it, but it would have to have been someone who knew the difference between proclaiming faith and being a person of true faith:

I was hungry,
  and you formed a humanities club
  to discuss my hunger.
I was imprisoned,
  and you crept off quietly to your chapel
  to pray for my release.
I was naked,
  and in your mind you debated the morality
  of my appearance.
I was sick,
  and you knelt and thanked God
  for your health.
I was homeless,
  and you preached to me of the spiritual shelter
  of the love of God.
I was lonely,
  and you left me alone
  to pray for me.
You seem so holy,
  so close to God.
But I'm still very hungry,
  and lonely,
  and cold.

Having faith is not an easy matter. It demands that we see Christ in everyone and follow the blueprint for life which he gave us in Matthew 25: "I was hungry and you fed me...in prison and you visited me...naked and you clothed me." But how many of us actually see the face of Christ in a hungry person or in a prisoner or in our neighbor? The nineteenth-century Russian author Ivan Turgenev wrote of a dream he had, of being young and in a small church:

All at once a man came up from behind and stood beside me. I did not turn towards him; but at once I felt that this man was Christ....[He had] a face like everyone's, a face like all men's faces...and the clothes on him like everyone's.

"What sort of Christ is this?" I thought. "Such an ordinary, ordinary man! It can't be!" I turned away.

And suddenly, my heart sank and I came to myself. Only then I realized that just such a face—a face like all men's faces—is the face of Christ.

As a Catholic journalist, I have occasionally covered stories of people who looked into another person's face and saw Christ. This one began with a thirty-three-year-old man named Hector, who came from Puerto Rico. He had traveled to New York State to visit his mother, recently remarried. And there something happened that turned the visit into one of those scary, ugly family incidents.

While at his mother's house, Hector went berserk, threatening to kill both his mother and his stepfather. Knowing Hector to be a man with a prison record and very familiar with guns, the couple had run from their house in terror, still in their nightclothes. Their screams started a commotion in the neighborhood.

Frightened, Hector barricaded himself in an upstairs bedroom of the house. Neighbors called the police, who surrounded the house cautiously, not knowing if or how heavily armed the young man might be. The police tried to talk him into leaving the house peacefully, but no way. Hector didn't trust that he would get out alive and told them so. His response was, "I want a priest."

The police went to the pastor of a nearby parish. It was around 10:00 PM. The pastor, who came to the door in casual clothes, was given details of the situation. The police then told him that they couldn't really ask him to come to the house because they believed Hector was armed, as well as irrational, unpredictable, and dangerous. They wanted the pastor to be fully aware of what he was risking if he went with them.

It turned out that this priest had actually worked with prisoners for a long time. He understood the language of the desperate, their angers and their fears. And so he simply said to the police, with good humor, "I'll be right with you, but first, let me dress for the occasion." Two minutes later he was back, having put on his roman collar, and they were on their way.

By this time, the neighborhood was literally hopping with excitement. This only made Hector more nervous as he crouched in the dark, half-hidden behind a desk which he had pushed to the open door. Because the police had told him they wouldn't get a priest unless they saw his empty hands, his hands were on the desk, empty and in sight.

The priest had to stand in the doorway in order to talk to Hector. He was directly in front of the distraught man, about four feet away, almost within touching distance. Framed by light from the hallway behind him, he was a perfect target—from both sides. A sharpshooter policeman was poised behind him, gun aimed, ready to let go should Hector make a sudden move with a weapon. As Father told me later, either way, it wasn't the greatest place to be standing.

The priest got Hector talking and immediately he launched into his complaints about "the system," and everything in his life that had gone wrong. He relayed his fears that the police would kill him or put him in jail. The priest reassured him he would be taken to the hospital to help him get his head straightened out.

While they were talking, Hector suddenly took his hands off the desk. The policeman behind Father screamed, "Put your hands on the desk!" The priest never flinched. He held out his hand. Hector got up. The police pounced on him with cuffs.

The priest stayed with the poor, sick man until he was admitted to the psychiatric unit of a nearby hospital. The next day, the police said that if the priest hadn't been there, Hector probably would have made a foolish move, the police would have had to open fire, and Hector would most likely be in a morgue, not a hospital.

We sometimes think that priests are safely secure in their rectories, out of touch with the hard reality of the daily, problem-laden lives of people. Yet once in a while, we are reminded of the heroic side of their lives, such as the times when they respond to an accident and have to administer last rites to a teenager in pieces, or stand between an unstable man and a police gun in the hope of saving one life.

I asked this priest why he was willing to risk his life for a stranger. The priest replied with his typical good humor, yet utterly serious: "He wasn't a stranger. Didn't you look at him? That was the face of Christ if I ever saw one." Anyone who was there that day saw faith alive, in action.

Love opens the door

Great faith is shown in far less dramatic ways most of the time. I have been privileged to see people reach out to others with little touches that say simply, but strongly, here is a person spreading love in his or her own "little way," to use the words of Thérèse of Lisieux.

Years ago an unexpected package arrived at my home. There was no note, only a return address, that of my Aunt Thelma. Inside the package was a beautiful, hand-crocheted afghan. I immediately called to thank her. She had recently been widowed after taking care of Uncle Don, who was blind and very ill for years. They never had the gift of children. She told me that her hope was to make an afghan for each niece, all nine of us, now that she had the time. It was a lovely, thoughtful, unexpected act of love, one that will be with me for the rest of my life.

Another time, when I was an editor for a weekly newspaper, I was working hard and late one afternoon. A young woman who worked in the production department suddenly stood at my door, holding a cup of water. She said she had noticed I hadn't been away from my desk for hours, and knew I must be thirsty. I recognized her in this little act of kindness. She was Christ.

If we could just see how pervasive the presence of God is in our world and in our lives, we wouldn't even have to talk about faith. We would be aware of God in every relationship, action, work, and in every breath. We would know without having to use words how loved we are because our eyes and our hearts would see and know this truth. The poet Walt Whitman had this vision. He wrote:

I see something of God each hour of the
Twenty-four, and each moment then.
In the faces of men and women I see God, and

In my own face in the glass.
I find letters from God dropped in the street,
And every one is signed by God's name.
And I leave them where they are, for I know
That wheresoe'er I go
Others will punctually come forever and ever.

One might cynically counter that, sure, God sends letters, but all too often they are full of bad news. The English writer C.S. Lewis addressed that reality in his book *Mere Christianity*, saying we shouldn't be surprised if we are in for a rough ride. He wrote:

When a man turns to Christ and seems to be getting on pretty well...he often feels that it would now be natural if things went fairly smoothly. When troubles come along—illnesses, money troubles, new kinds of temptation—he is disappointed...why now? Because God is forcing him on, or up, to a higher level; putting him into situations where he will have to be very much braver, or more patient, or more loving, than he ever dreamed of being before. It seems to us all unnecessary; but that is because we have not yet had the slightest notion of the tremendous thing he means to make of us.

And then, in one of the most memorable passages Lewis wrote, he gives us a parable, comparing each of us to a "living house" that God has come into to rebuild. At first, every remodeling he takes on makes sense.

But presently he starts knocking the house about in a way that hurts abominably and does not seem to make sense. What on earth is he up to? The explanation is that he is building quite a different house from the one you thought of....You thought you were going to be made into a decent little cottage; but he is building a palace. He intends to come and live in it himself.

If we could remember this parable and believe it, our faith would never falter. More than that, we would try to get everyone we know to see what God is trying to make of us—his dwelling place—and why this can't happen unless we journey through a process that requires pounding, nailing, cutting, and polishing, a rebuilding, remodeling job we can reduce to two words, suffering and pain.

As for why it has to be this way, we can only repeat over and over: we really don't know. The answer lies in God's realm. All we know for sure is that there is a connection between suffering and our destination, which is to become one with the Father in heaven and share in his glory. Jesus spent his life trying to help us grasp this message, to accept suffering and death as he did, even if we are innocent, as he was. Yet even as God, the builder, is pounding away at us, the beauty he is creating can come through. Here is what Gandhi said in one of his meditations:

It is by my fetters that I can fly,
It is by my sorrows that I can soar,
It is by my reverses that I can run,
It is by my tears that I can travel,
It is by my cross that I can climb
Into the heart of humanity.

Gandhi says, as Jesus lived, that the great meaning of suffering is to teach us compassion for others. If our feelings never come to life, we remain sterile. If we feel love we can feel pain, and love is never sterile. With love we yearn to be connected to others, to be one with everything created and with the Creator. This is the mansion God is building of us, the one he wants to live in.

Love, then, opens the door to faith. But how do we practice love? That was the question answered by the late Fulton Oursler, the great writer and Catholic convert. He wrote,

It is so easy for one to give a coin or write a check against peoples' misery. But love is not giving money. It is giving myself. I must minister with my own hands, reach out and give some personal help to someone, not just occasionally, but every day. And I must go out of my way to do it, not in the mood of a Lord Bountiful, but with tenderness. Such love begins with the person who is nearest to me at this moment; it knows no end, anywhere. All living responds to tenderness. The potency of love and faith has transformed my life. In them lies my only true security.

It is evident that the greatest enemy of faith is self-centeredness. One cannot nourish a relationship—especially where oneness with all other created beings is essential—when self comes first. If we accept that faith is a relationship with Jesus, our acceptance requires action. We will have to ask how this relationship can be manifested. The good news is that Jesus gave us a detailed blueprint for how to work out the relationship between him and us. It is all in his lesson summed up in these words: "Truly I tell you, just as you did it to one of the least of these who are members of my family, you did it to me" (Mt 25:40).

Faith is intrinsically bound up with how we treat one another, and how we care about others is intrinsically bound up with the battle between selfishness and love. Each of us must discover for ourselves how to feed the hungry, give drink to the thirsty, forgive enemies, and do good to those who persecute us. Each of us must discover for ourselves what it means to love, to be just, to be a peacemaker. That is the challenge of faith.

It has been said often that "the heart is a hunger." Indeed, if the heart isn't fed, we suffer a terrible malnutrition. Paradoxically, the heart is fed not by consuming but by giving. A Protestant woman in an interfaith group told me a story that really pointed this out:

An old Chinese man, about to die, was visited by the Angel of Death, who asked him, "Where do you prefer to go—heaven or hell?" The old man replied, "I don't know what either place is like. Show me so I can make a wise choice."

So the Angel took the old man to hell—and hell was a beautiful dining room, with tables laden down with luxurious foods. The people, however, were sitting starved and emaciated. "'Why don't they eat?" asked the old man, bewildered. "There's a rule here," the Angel answered, pointing a finger at the tables and explaining, "They can only eat by using those chopsticks." It was then the old man saw—the chopsticks were six feet long!

The Angel then took the old man to heaven. To his surprise, he saw that heaven was the identical dining hall, only here the people were well fed, smiling and happy. He looked at the Angel, smiled knowingly and said, "Ah—here they have different rules." The Angel said no, again pointing to six-foot-long chopsticks, and replied, "But here, they feed one another."

This is only a story, but it so well expresses the truth that faith is not something to hold to ourselves. If it were, it could only shrivel and die. Faith cannot be static, cannot be clutched to ourselves; that is as intrinsically impossible as it is to draw a square circle. Faith is a life-giving energy, and the more it is shared, the more it is generated.

When I was a sophomore at the College of St. Rose in Albany, New York, we gathered for our annual three-day retreat. The priest that year was contagiously enthusiastic about how privileged we all were to have been baptized in this great Christian faith. He had a running theme throughout his talks that has stayed with me during all the years that have followed. He said, "Young women, when you leave here, don't keep the faith. Spread the faith."

This priest wanted us to see that faith is not a gift to be kept but a dynamic, living way of life to be expressed in all our relationships for the rest of our lives. A tall order? You bet. But I think he got the word straight from the boss.

CHAPTER NINE

Touching Heaven

If we haven't found God on earth, we won't find him in heaven. For heaven's not some other world where we go to escape; the kingdom of heaven's already in us, and we have to build it up with the graces God gives us.

▶ LOUIS EVELY

The word "heaven" is constantly sprinkled into conversation. If we are enjoying ourselves, we say we are in heaven. We worry that if we misbehave, we won't go to heaven. Things like ice cream and coffee are called "heavenly." Songs tell us that "heaven can wait..." and preachers say "prepare for heaven now."

Really, no one could argue that heaven doesn't get enough mention. And yet heaven may be the most misunderstood word in our language because now we see "through a glass darkly," as Paul writes in his first letter to the Corinthians (13).

Part of the reason may rest in the gospels themselves. When Jesus sends out his seventy disciples to carry his message to every town and place, he tells them upon their return to "rejoice and be glad, for your reward is great in heaven." He exhorts his followers to "seek first the kingdom of heaven" and "lay up for yourselves treasures in heaven." In his parables, Jesus often begins, "The kingdom of heaven is like...." Indeed, heaven sounds like a destination to be reached, like taking a trip to New York or London.

From the time we were children, if someone asked where we wanted to go at the end of life, most of us would have answered, "I want to go to heaven." We may still answer that way. Many of us see heaven as a blissful site located in a Utopia up in the sky where everything is perfect—in contrast to hell, where nasty demons grind their teeth and poor souls get barbecued for being really, really bad.

Well, it is long past time to put aside these old notions of heaven and hell. Shortly before proclaiming the year 2000 as the Great Jubilee, Pope John Paul II sketched out a different and surprisingly modern picture of life after death. Heaven and hell, he said, are not places at all but "states of being," and the best way to imagine them is to "reflect on significant spiritual moments in this life— the pain brought on by sin, and the happiness experienced when doing good."

The pontiff emphasized that it is absolutely wrong to think of heaven as the place where God is found. "God simply cannot be confined by such a concept...(for heaven) is neither an abstraction nor a place in the clouds, but a living, personal relationship with the Trinity." As for hell, the pope said that the language of "unquenchable fire" should be seen as symbolic. He explained, "Hell is not the punishment of an angry God but a self-imposed exile by people who have used their freedom to say 'no' to God."

Thus, we have it straight from the pope that the determining factor for being either eternally separated from God or eternally happy with God is one solitary thing: human choice. Commenting on the pope's statements about heaven and hell, Msgr. Inos Biffi, an Italian theologian, said the pope was hinting that "the person who lives in grace already lives in paradise." What a comforting thought that is. Certainly it is true that the pope, in his wisdom, radically reaffirmed the true definition of heaven given to us by Jesus in Luke 17: "The kingdom of God does not come in such a way as to be seen. No one will say, 'Look, here it is! There it is!' Because the kingdom of God is within you."

Back in the early 1990s, I interviewed Rev. F. Newton Howden, an Episcopal priest who had written a book about the afterlife. He, too, had come to understand that heaven is not a place.

> If we must localize heaven at all, perhaps it would be correct to say that heaven is all around us, for it breaks in upon us from time to time....The most accurate, general statement we can make about heaven is that it is an intensification of the best that a Christian can know and do and believe during this life.

Much earlier, back in the 1960s, Louis Evely had also written, insistently, that heaven was not a destination. Eternal life begins on earth, he stated.

> Earth is a place where we build our heaven. God doesn't invite us to pass into the next world. Rather, He's invited Himself into this world; He's redeemed it and released into it infinite forces which He's entrusted to us so that we might transform it; and someday He'll crown His work and ours by making it eternal.

Evely commented on people who say they want to be a saint after they die. He scoffed in a way, remarking that if you are not a saint before you die, you will surely never become one afterwards. Life, not death, determines who you are and whether the part of earth you touch has become a heaven. Like it or not, life itself is the testing ground where we eventually make the crucial choice: self-love or heaven.

Heaven here and now

Every life is filled with incidents I call "moments of truth" where we have a choice to act either in self-interest or in concern for another. In effect, this creates a bit of heaven or hell here and now.

When the pope asked us to look back over our lives for significant spiritual moments where we brought goodness or harm to this earth, I recalled an incident from my childhood that momentarily gave me a taste of hell and forever changed how I would treat another person.

It happened when I was in the fourth grade. That year one of the boys in my class was extremely disruptive. He wasn't noisy or cruel; in fact, he was very quiet. He dressed shabbily, wearing the same clothes for weeks on end, and they often emitted an unpleasant odor. I was too unsophisticated at the time to realize he was probably poor and neglected.

Besides his physical attributes, he had a way of doing things that was disruptive to the teacher, who would sometimes tell him he was in for a lot of trouble if he didn't stop his sneaky ways.

Then one day the boy came to school very late and was escorted to class by the principal. In front of the whole class, she gave him a little speech about discipline. Then, surprisingly, she asked us outright what we thought of our classmate. Hands shot up and as the principal acknowledged them, one by one his faults were listed: "He steals my homework." "He talks back to the teacher." "He tells lies." "He chews gum in class." "He stays too long in the boy's room."

And on and on. I sat there, wanting to be part of the action, racking my nine-year-old brain to see what complaint I could come up with. I didn't want to be outdone by the others. Then I had it. I raised my hand. The principal nodded my way and I said, "He always scratches the blackboard with the chalk and laughs when it makes us shiver."

The boy looked at me with the same fixed smile he had worn all the while he had been on the chopping block. I was suddenly ashamed for what I had said. Just then the principal said softly, "I let all you children talk about him because I was waiting—hoping—to see if anyone, just one of you, would say something nice about him." Her words stunned me, and my shame at having so eagerly joined in the beating burned into me permanently.

That night I couldn't sleep. I cried for a long time because I had been so cruel to another person. I kept wondering how I would have felt if I had been that boy. It was only much later, as I grew in my faith, that I realized Jesus would have set me straight, letting me know I was he, indeed, for we are all one. To this day my tongue becomes paralyzed if I have to say something which I think is going to hurt another person. And that is good. This pause buys time, forcing me to examine honestly if my need to act is truly necessary, reminding me to pray a moment for God's help.

The letters "WWJD," which mean "What would Jesus do?" have become a popular logo in recent years, and are often seen on bracelets and other objects. This question, "what would Jesus do?" is one we should always ask, for if we did so and acted on the answer, we would be surrounded by heaven.

I will repeat what I have said earlier. There is only one way we can build heaven on this earth, by following the blueprint Jesus so clearly spelled out in Matthew 25:31–40: "I was hungry and you fed me...." These words challenge us to ask the always uncomfortable question—how do we serve others?

Not long ago, a letter crossed my desk in which a writer asked for help in "living the true Christian faith." He expressed a sense of frustration because it appeared to him that opportunities for good, useful, volunteer work were hard to find in our affluent society. I think his problem was that he had not come to understand who the poor really are and how we can serve them. The hard truth is that we will never discover heaven if we don't do the work of Christ in a society where need is so often camouflaged.

Who are Christ's poor, anyway? Certainly there are the visible poor: the thousands who died this very day because of malnutrition; the tenement dwellers in inner cities; the mentally retarded whose poverty is the deprivation of normal intellectual gifts; the emotionally and psychologically disturbed people whose poverty is the lack of the innate equipment needed to cope with life. There are also the invisible poor, including those who live with disappointment and frustration because their deepest hopes for their lives have not been realized.

Jesus recognized that poverty is a condition of humankind. His statement about this has remained controversial to this day: "You always have the poor with you" (Jn 12:8). In no way do these words imply we should ignore the poor. On the contrary, Jesus gave us the formula for coping with poverty, that is, to feed the hungry and clothe the naked and visit the imprisoned.

The message is crystal clear. When we respond to the needs of another, we make Jesus present once more in the world. The formula given by Jesus is an affirmation of human solidarity: our solidarity in suffering, our solidarity in helping one another, and ultimately, our solidarity in the redemption which begins right here on earth. In grasping this truth and acting on it we achieve our salvation, heaven, or our destruction, hell, long before we take our last breath.

I once had the privilege of interviewing theologian Harvey Cox, a man of wisdom. He spoke of how an affluent society can so easily ignore the poor. "We are now in a stage where we are so insulated from each other, from the hard facts of life, that unless you make intentional efforts to involve yourself and your children in the agony of humanity, it won't happen," he said. In other words, if we shut out the poor, the hungry, the naked, those in prison, and those in pain from any cause, we not only insulate ourselves from them, but from heaven as well.

The man who wrote me the letter mentioned earlier in this chapter used the word "affluent." This word implies we have an abundance to share. But do we realize that feeding the hungry also means asking for a welfare program that aims not just at survival of the poor but also tries to maintain the dignity of those in need? Can we understand that our abundance includes our education, our technical know-how, our agriculture, our conservation and planning expertise that can be shared with developing nations?

Can we accept the fact that serving others is often done by attending boring meetings to vote against construction of a nuclear power plant or a wireless tower in a heavily populated area; to vote for zoning changes that will allow low-cost housing to be built; to seek help for pregnant adolescent girls; to plan parish programs that support good educational programs which strengthen

Christian values? The list of ways we help those in need is endless, if we really think about it.

The only way I can respond to a person who is asking for help in living the true Christian faith is to express my belief that first, we must see the face of God in everyone. We cannot be Christians on our own terms; it has to be done on the terms of the world in which we live and of the people who share this world with us.

The ways we live out the Christian faith can run the gamut from taking in and caring for a homeless child, to working for a political candidate who will underscore legislation that insures social justice. In all cases, the energy that allows us to roll up our sleeves and work for the good of others is a belief in the message of Jesus, the vision to see where the work lies, and the love that leads to our resounding "yes." Best of all, there is a prize for all this work. It is heaven.

Circle of life

Given all the evil, heartache, loss, and disaster which we deal with constantly, it is not easy to hold to the truth that God is with us here in our physical lifetimes. When I tell people that even though pain and suffering exists the earth is permeated with the presence of God, I often receive a sarcastic response: "God who?" for example. These are the times when I wish I were more eloquent so I could paint a vivid word-picture of the God I have come to see in this incredible world.

One early morning a few years back, I was on my way to Mass at a nearby monastery when the sun made its appearance, gloriously. It wasn't brilliant silver on this morning, forcing you to look away. Rather, it was muted gold, allowing me to steal some long glances at it. That morning, the sun was a perfect circle, so breathtakingly awesome that all I could do was catch my breath, giving praise and thanks to the Lord. Watching that presence, encircled with a divine mystery, I wondered how anyone could ever doubt the existence of the Creator, and how truly he had left his trademark in ways such as the sun.

Later at Mass, I was still thinking of the sun when the priest raised the host at the consecration. Again I saw a circle.

This dual vision of the circle-sun and the circle-host filled me with awe, and I remembered what a priest once told me about how he viewed circles. A circle is a perfect symbol for God, he said, for it has no beginning and no end. I remembered, too, that Augustine had linked the circle to God. In one of his essays, Ralph Waldo Emerson had reminded us of this, writing, "St. Augustine described the nature of God as a circle whose centre was everywhere and its circumference nowhere."

Before that day was over, I meditated a lot on how the symbolism of circles is really quite pervasive, especially as it relates to the perpetuation of God-given life. For example, trees and vegetation are shade and food, but they begin with a seed—which is a circle. The smallest particle of life is the cell—which is a circle. The fertilized egg that becomes a baby is a circle. And the eye, which internalizes all the wonders of creation, is a circle. The earth itself, when seen from outer space, is a circle.

I don't think the Creator came up with the design of the circle by accident. I think it was God's way of getting us to see that when it comes to the origins and regeneration of life, there is no beginning and no end. All is contained within himself, the perfect circle.

I have always been blown away by Jesus's prayer to his Father just before he was to be taken away and murdered: "I in them and you in me, that they may become completely one, so that the world may know that you have sent me and have loved them even as you have loved me" (Jn 17:23). I believe Jesus was describing the circle of love that is creation.

Even the American Indians knew that the mystery of creation was contained in the circle. In a famous book called *Black Elk Speaks: Being the Life Story of a Holy Man of the Oglala Sioux*, the author writes: "Everything an Indian does is in a circle, and that is because the power of the world always works in circles, and everything tries to be round. Even the seasons form a great circle in their changing, and always come back again where they were."

For anyone struggling with an elusive faith, doubting the existence of the Creator, I would say, look at the circle in the sky and see the reminder of how gracious a Host we earthly pilgrims have. For anyone doubting that earth is filled with heaven, I would urge them to look at the circles that fill our universe, the trademarks of the Creator who has no beginning and no end. I simply have to believe that God designed everything with the mark of the circle so we could see the signs of his presence among us, around us, within us, and above us.

Even a secular scientist could express wonder at the earth. The late Dr. Lewis Thomas, who headed Memorial Sloan-Kettering Cancer Center in New York City, wrote a book called *The Lives of a Cell*. This book was truly a celebration of life, and it won the National Book Award in 1974.

I had the privilege of meeting Dr. Thomas and interviewing him when I was on the staff of the State University of New York at Stony Brook. He was at the university because he had been invited to be the guest speaker for the first graduating class of medical students. I couldn't wait to get a copy of his book, and when I read it, some of his reflections astounded me, like this one:

> I have been trying to think of the earth as a kind of organism, but it is no go. I cannot think of it this way. It is too big, too complex....The other night driving through a hilly, wooded part of southern New England, I wondered about this. If not an organism, what is it like, what is it most like? Then, satisfactory for that moment, it came to me: it is most like a single cell.

Imagine. The very earth itself, most like a single cell, the unit that contains the origins of life. A circle—God's trademark! Here is another observation of Dr. Thomas:

> Viewed from the distance of the moon, the astonishing thing about the earth, catching the breath, is that it is alive. Aloft, floating free beneath the moist, gleaming membrane of bright blue sky, is the rising earth, the only exuberant thing in this part of the cosmos.
>
> If you had been looking for a very long, geologic time, you

could have seen the continents themselves in motion, drifting apart on their crustal plates, held afloat by the fire beneath. It has the organized, self-contained look of a live creature, full of information, marvelously skilled in handling the sun.

I call his words an ode to the Creator, who has put his life into the world he made and gave to us, an earth he infuses with life forever. God has literally given us "an appetite for the Infinite," as Beatrice Bruteau, a scholar, contemplative, writer, and long-time dear friend of mine puts it. Conscious of God's vibrating creation, she writes:

After a while we become aware that praying is going on. The earth is praying, the rocks, the ground, the grass, the trees, the distant rivers and the sea. The heavens are praying, the slender heavens and all the stars. The awareness of the reality, the presence and the dearness of God is becoming palpable. The prayer of all the world lifts gently around us, like a great heart beating, like a giant breath rising and falling in rhythm. The prayer penetrates and permeates us. We rest in it and let it fill us.

It is God's love. God's love in the earth, God's love in Jesus and in us. This is what we are, all of us; we are made of God's love, breathing and beating. We become keenly aware of being made by and out of this pulsating divine presence. We are resting on the groundwork of reality in God's love.

When we open our eyes and our hearts and see that God is truly present in this world, then we move out any darkness that prevents us from seeing heaven is always within our reach. Once we recognize God is everywhere, then we begin to have a new faith, one full of wonder, ever more challenging than we might want. For while heaven *comes* without our invitation, simply out of the goodness and love of God, it cannot *stay* without our invitation. We have to earn our heaven day by day, living and working according to the blueprint of Jesus. And the only time we can to do this is now.

Infinite joy

We can always know if we are touching heaven; Jesus himself gave us the clue. On the very eve of his crucifixion, he said to his apostles, "These things I have spoken to you that my joy may be in you, and that your joy may be filled." Here is a man about to be arrested, beaten, spit upon, cursed, humiliated, and killed, and he is talking about joy! Jesus was expressing a paradox, that one can be unhappy from suffering enormous injustice, loss, and pain, yet still be joyful, because joy is our connection to something bigger than ourselves, something magnificent. Could there be anything more important?

Here is something else: Jesus didn't use the word "happiness." He said "joy." The word "joy" appears over and over again in the New Testament, some fifty times, always in connection with receiving the good news. Joy means we have touched God. When we know joy, we know heaven.

I first had a glimpse of joy when I was an eighth grader many decades ago. It happened about a week before Christmas, a time when my mood was bubbly because I loved preparing for this greatest of all seasons. I had stayed late at school one day that week, and so did a boy about my age. It happened that we met in the hallway and struck up a conversation for the first time. He had been a new student that September, and he was black, a newcomer from St. Peter Claver's in "the colored part of the city," the only one of his ethnic background in the school. This was long before the civil rights movement had taken off and my city, like all others, had its well defined walls of insulation for whites.

The boy was polite and shy. As we talked, I felt embarrassed, even ashamed, that I had never gone out of my way to welcome him before. I wondered how many, if any, of the other kids had. We talked a bit about Christmas, and then he startled me by saying, "Sometimes at night I pray that I'll wake up white." I felt his utter loneliness and I understood a glimmer of it, for I was Italian, a minority in a mostly-Irish school. I remember telling him, "Sometimes I pray that I'll wake up Irish."

At that moment one of the Sisters came by. There was no intentional unkindness in her, but we both got the message when she said, "Antoinette, you shouldn't be seen with him." He answered very softly, "Don't worry, Sister. I'm not coming back after Christmas." She walked away.

I felt uncomfortable about what he had said. "But why...?" I didn't finish my question. We looked at each other. We both knew why. And then something happened, maybe to both of us. I knew calmly and solidly and instantly that I would never pray to wake up Irish again. I said aloud to him, "Please, say a different prayer tonight." He smiled, and it was different—so different that again something happened. I didn't feel bubbly anymore, but in a quiet way I was soaring. Somehow this boy and I had traveled very suddenly from strangers to friends. We had connected and we were new people. I felt joy.

That is when I learned for the first time that joy is an aftermath. Joy comes after there has been a connection between persons which brings to each a moment of pure understanding and unity. This is the kind of relationship that is forever "Christmas"; that is, the eruption of love on earth that lifts humans to a God-level.

I never saw the boy again, but that day I made a pledge to work to end the separation between blacks and whites, and I have kept that pledge ever since. This is work where I have seen the hand of God and it has brought me the greatest joy.

When I use the word joy, I want to make it clear that I am not talking about happiness. We tend to mix these words as if they are synonymous, but they are not. Happiness can be defined as pleasure, contentment, gladness, favored by fortune, or delighted. Happiness comes from the attainment of what one considers to be good. Most of the time, happiness has to be earned; you have to work at it.

Joy is different. It goes beyond happiness and exists on a different plane. Joy can be defined as exultant satisfaction, great gladness, rejoicing, or bliss. We have to experience joy to know the difference between joy and happiness.

I once took on the task of interviewing people to find out, "When were you happy?" Here are some of the answers they gave:

when I got a job, passed a test, remodeled the house, went to a good show, made a great meal, and so on.

Then I surprised them by changing the question, asking "When were you joyful?" The answers didn't come as quickly as the answers to the first question. But when they would start to talk, I heard something different. People were joyful...when my baby was born, when I fell in love, finished a sculpture, wrote a book, volunteered at hospice (or other ways of helping someone else), and so forth.

It became clear to me that the responses to the question "When were you happy?" were all earthy. But the answers to "When were you joyful?" showed that joy was linked to something bigger than self. Joy clearly had to do with being linked to the loving creativity of the Creator. This reminded me of a banner I had in the house when my children were young. It said, "Joy is the sign of God in you." This means that joy is the wonderful state of being where we are connected to the spirit of the universe—God. Joy has to do with love.

Joy is permanent, while happiness often comes with a sense of unease and worry. Happiness raises concerns like "how long will this last?" or "when will the spell be broken?" Happiness has its roots in passing things, and so will pass when they do. Not so joy.

Jesus teaches that we were made to have joy because joy is linked to heaven. What this means is that no matter what happens to us here, no matter how many losses we are hit with, no matter how broken we are or how mired in grief, we can still be filled with joy because joy results from our connection with the eternal. Therefore it too must be eternal.

Yet joy is a paradox because we can only reach that higher spiritual connection through our bodies and this world. It is precisely those difficult, human conditions which force us to find a new meaning for life, and this can put us on the path of joy. As William Wordsworth wrote, "With the deep power of joy, we see into the God of things." Imagine that! The God of things. Could the truth of all we are and all we have be better put than that?

Theologian Hans Küng points out,

The "heaven of Christian faith" is not a place where God sits in his "throne room." No, the naïve anthropomorphic idea of a heaven above the clouds can no longer be revived. God does not dwell as "supreme being" in a local or spatial sense "above" the world, in a "world above." Christians believe God is in the world.

Our faith gives us an incredible understanding of God, who cannot be localized somewhere in space but is always within our reach, one with us all while ever mysterious. The focus of our faith should be to bring what we can of heaven to this earth. Then, when our earthly journey ends, we will be in familiar territory, now luminous beyond anything we could now imagine.

Louis Evely affirmed this:

The biggest surprise about heaven'll be that there's nothing new there. When we wake up from this long sleep and all its nightmares, we'll find ourselves clasped in the same arms that have always held us. The glorious face that'll beam down on us in tenderness and joy will be the one we've always sensed was watching over us in our trials and sorrows.

At long last, we'll recognize the elusive but faithful friend whose mysterious presence puzzled us.

CHAPTER TEN

Staying Faith-full

We cannot fall into nothingness, for our lives are rooted in the absolute. We're on loan, leased out to an earthly existence for a span of years, hungering and thirsting for our return to God.

▶ JAMES M. SOMERVILLE

During his time on this earth, Jesus offered the people—and us—an invitation to inner growth. He didn't talk about original sin, rules and regulations, religious packages, formulas, or pat answers. His whole life declared that the way for human beings to save themselves is to grow into the fullness of their powers, knowing that the greatest of these powers is love. This was the message that came from the one who said he was the son and God was his father. Then as now, this message is for all people, both those who have faith and those who do not.

First, however, we must understand what it is Christ is asking of us, and there is only one way to find that out. We have to look at Jesus' life with our minds and with our hearts. And what will we find? No matter how often I read the gospels and reflect on the life and words of Jesus, I keep coming back to one conclusion. He did not ask us to be heroic, or to be perpetually on our knees. He asked us to become mature in the same way he was.

Think about this. Jesus saw his own people defeated twice, first by the brutality of the Romans, as well as by the greedy power of individuals and groups like the scribes and the Pharisees; but secondly, by their own inability to rise above the power of those who mastered them. Jesus' people envied those in power even while they hated them. They imitated their authoritative ways when possible, believing that happiness could only come through methods employed by the people in power. (Many biblical historians believe this was the mindset of Judas, who felt betrayed after Jesus made it clear that when he talked of salvation, he wasn't referring to military victory.)

With his Godly sense of life, Jesus tried to get the people to see that true happiness would come only when the patterns of earthly power were rejected. Listen to some of the things he said in this regard: "Blessed are the meek.... He who loses his life shall find it.... It is more blessed to give than to receive.... Blessed are the peacemakers.... Do unto others as you would have others do unto you."

Even when it came to paying taxes, Jesus didn't get uptight. Remember when the taxman went after Jesus and his disciples? This story remains one of the classic jokes in history. It took an original thinker, someone who could see the fun in a practical joke, to tell Peter to pull a fish out of the water, open its mouth, and in it he would find the tax money (Mt 17:24–27). I love this story. I believe it shows Jesus making the point that maturity means you accept responsibility—paying taxes falls into that category—and that maturity also requires a sense of humor.

Jesus' message was in sharp contrast to what the drummers of that time were playing. Jesus changed the score. He asked the people to listen to a different drummer—a Master Drummer. He asked people to hear his truth and follow him, to understand faith according to a new definition, one related to the Father and to the son and to others. Could we stay faithful—that is, full of faith—in the darkness, in dry seasons, when plunged into loss, pain, and near despair? That was the challenge he put before us.

Jesus was saying that the person who listens to him, who understands him and chooses to join him in this new maturity, will be able to discern which messages are from false prophets and which are from righteous drummers. He invited us to join him, to form a relationship with him, to be full of faith—faithful.

Our faith challenge today is different from anything we have known in the past because we are in a new era of mass communication, so pervasive it is called an "age"—the Information Age. We are inundated with messages brought to us by the latest technology, be it digital, wireless, or the internet. The discordant drums of technology may be playing different tunes, but most of them are giving us consumer messages of one kind or another. (This even comes out of the mouths of babes. At Christmastime I was in a store, and overheard Santa ask a child what he wanted for Christmas. "Everything on Channel 10," answered the child, who had already internalized the consumer message.)

The trouble with consumer messages gone to extremes is that they basically contradict Jesus' call to maturity. Consumerism is self-focused and the more we turn inward, the smaller we get. As the saying goes, "A person all wrapped up in self makes a mighty small package." Self-centeredness is the great enemy of faith. After all, how can one nourish a relationship—with God or with anybody—when self comes first?

That question is crucial. If we accept that faith is a relationship with Christ, we have to ask how this relationship can be manifested. Faith is intrinsically bound up with how we treat one another, and how we care about others is intrinsically bound up with the battle between selfishness and love. I say this again, because it is the core of faith: each of us must discover how to feed the hungry, give drink to the thirsty, forgive enemies, and do good to those who persecute us. Each of us must discover what it means to love, to be just, to be a peacemaker. Most often this discovery comes after a blow that shatters our comfort and compels us to break out of our self-focused ways.

People of faith
I once read an article about the actor Martin Sheen, who had "abandoned" his Catholic roots, as he put it, for many years. After

an emotional breakdown at the age of forty-one, he came back to the Church. He has made headlines ever since primarily because he is outspoken about his faith and demonstrates it in activism, from protesting toxic waste leaks to marching against the presence of nuclear weapons. Sheen said in the article:

> The miracle is God chooses us. That's the hardest part to accept. A child gets it. A simple person gets it. You get intellectual and you can't get it. God chooses to come through us. That's the miracle. I don't want to wake up one day and realize that I've spent all my time in the future or the past. I think that life is such a wonderful mystery. Even when it's tough, it's a wonderful journey, and it's filled with great, great adventures, large and small, always human. I wouldn't change at thing.

That could be the testimony only of a person of faith.

Actor/dancer Ben Vereen, who reached the top when he starred on Broadway in *Jesus Christ Superstar* and *Pippin*, gave a strong declaration of faith after he came close to death in 1992. Vereen had been struck by a car while walking near his California home, and he called what he learned from his suffering a "new day." In an interview a few years after his accident, he said,

> The way I see it, since the accident was in 1992, I'll be four years old in 1996. I'm so grateful; I've got another chance to get it right. Religion, to me, is needed, and what we were taught to think of as blind faith isn't blind at all. What it is is visualizing.

Another testimony of faith that touched me came from Sr. Thea Bowman, an incredible shooting star who died from cancer at fifty-three in 1990. In the early 1980s we were both speakers at a faith gathering put on by the Archdiocese of St. Paul, Minnesota. The highlight of the weekend was my encounter with Sr. Thea, who presented a concert called "God's Family Is a Rainbow," a combination of wisdom, spirituality, poetry, rhythm, love, and life. Sr. Thea communicated joy. She was blessed with the most beautiful singing voice I think I have ever heard.

Shortly before she died, I saw her on television being interviewed by Mike Wallace, I felt, as he did, enchanted by her, and wondered why God would take someone from this earth who had so much to give. But that is not for us to know, of course.

Sr. Thea remained a faith-teacher to the end. She said,

Perhaps suffering stops us in our tracks and forces us to confront what is real within us and in our environment. [Now] my faith is simpler. In many ways, it's easier; it's closer to home and reality. God is bread when you're hungry, water when you're thirsty, a harbor from the storm. God's a father to the fatherless, a mother to the motherless. God's my sister, my brother, leader, guide, teacher, comforter, friend.

God's the way-maker and burden-bearer, a heart fixer and mind regulator...God is my all in all, my everything...my rock, sword, shield, lily of the valley, pearl of great price.

And she gave added words of encouragement to sufferers: "Hold on just a little while longer. Everything is going to be all right." Truly, this was a woman who became ever more faith-full to the end of her life.

My father, Joseph Oppedisano, was my main teacher when it came to understanding that the root of faith is kindness to others. Like most Italian men of his generation, he didn't go to church very often, but he didn't doubt God. One of the first articles I ever wrote was about my father, published in 1953 in *The Apostle*, a Catholic magazine. I called it "Faith and a Smile." His faith in life and his smile were blessings I felt at a young age, and they sustained him for his eighty-three years on earth.

Dad was a butcher, and in my young teen years I worked with him in his store. He would say things I never forgot, like, "Antoinette, all that's important is a clear conscience and a big family." I especially remember how he would say to me, and later to my brothers who worked with him, "Don't ever turn anybody away." I saw that kindness over and over again. Countless people through the years walked out of his store with bags of food paid for with only a thank-you.

My father was only thirteen when he left his home in Calabria, Italy to try to make a life in the new country. When I think of him at that young age, heading north through Italy and France, trying to survive with no money and no skills, not knowing the language and with a war going on—this was 1915—I feel tremendous admiration for the strength he must have found to pursue his goal to get to the United States.

He remained in France for three years while he worked to earn enough money for a boat passage to the United States, and when he was sixteen, he finally made it over. When he arrived at Ellis Island, he thanked God for helping him get to the land of "gold." This was the beginning of his new life. He worked hard, learned the butcher trade, married a beautiful young woman named Mary, started his business, and raised a family of eight children. He never spoke of the U.S. without calling it "the best country in the world."

My father once told me that while he was living in France, working to earn his passage to America, he found himself starving. For the first and only time in his life, he stole something—a loaf of bread. "That's why," he said, "if anyone comes into my store hungry, I can't refuse them." He always gave with a smile. From his own pain, he had learned compassion.

I always remembered our dad's generosity, but it was my brother Joe who remembered the spindle. When my father died, Joe told the hundreds of relatives and friends who came to my father's funeral this story:

> Today, business has its ultra-sophisticated ways of keeping track of who owes how much money. But in those days, in our store, we had the spindle. We impaled pieces of paper on it each night, on which were recorded the cash register reading and the change count in the coin drawers.
>
> Then there were other scraps of paper on the spindle, each one containing a customer's name and varying dollar amounts. These slips represented people in the hurtful and uncomfortable position of having too much month left at the

end of their money. Sometimes the spindle would be thick with these "credit" notes. But more often than not, many of those slips with the names of people and the amounts owed would somehow become curiously missing, or would turn up as crumpled papers to be thrown out with the trash.

God uses his own measuring stick to evaluate his creatures. And I understand that if you observe very carefully, you will see that this [measuring stick] looks suspiciously like a gigantic, cosmic spindle to which are fastened all of those curiously lost and crumpled papers of our dad's life, each one convertible into some shining, celestial building material.

One day, when we join our dad, we shouldn't be surprised to find that he has one of the largest and most magnificent mansions among the many mansions Jesus said are in his Father's house.

None of us will ever, ever forget the story of the spindle, or how truly it symbolized my father's way of following Jesus' blueprint for living.

I learned even more from my father in his old age, that he had an incredible capacity to bear his own pain and that he refused to be a burden to anyone. I never heard him complain, not once, of his hurts and discomforts. His strength turned inward and the man who, in his younger years, was authoritative, forceful, and always in charge, became a truly gentle man, living simply, asking nothing, making no demands, quietly and strongly moving into his final journey.

My last memory of my father is of him strapped to his hospital bed, his arms slightly outstretched, his feet together. Feebly, he waved his hand from the wrist and gave me a broad smile before I left him. At that moment, I saw him as Jesus on his cross.

We buried him on a day that was cloudy and gray, wet from rain. But as my seven brothers and sisters and I simultaneously placed our flowers on his coffin at the cemetery, we were suddenly surrounded with light. The sun came out with the full glory of new life, and a gorgeous rainbow filled the sky. I was awed but not surprised, for I had always felt rainbows may be a sign of connection with loved ones who had died. After all, rainbows have a sacred meaning all the way back to the Book of Genesis, when God told Noah that the rainbow would be the sign of the covenant established between himself and every living thing found on earth.

God said, "I have set my bow in the clouds, and it shall be a sign of the covenant between me and the earth....When the bow is in the clouds, I will see it and remember the everlasting covenant between God and every living creature of all flesh that is on the earth" (Gen 9:13,16). When the sun and the rainbow appeared, we simply knew dad was smiling at us yet rejoicing in his Easter with the Lord. He wasn't really gone. He was with us and would be always. We had tears in our eyes but we were filled with joy.

That is a paradox of faith, that one can be overwhelmed with joy while immersed in pain. Jesus told us this was so. Even as he knew he would soon be arrested and put to death, he told his apostles, "I have said these things to you so that my joy may be in you, and that your joy may be complete....Love one another as I have loved you" (Jn 15:10–11). People who hear this, believe it, and live by it will always remain faith-full.

The light of love

I have emphasized in this book that faith is a relationship; it goes both ways. Yet how often have we really recognized that God is faithful, too, providing us with light for our journey, wanting only that we respond to his gifts with the simplicity of a child?

I often remember a story I heard some years ago, from a woman I had known earlier in life. Gloria and I were classmates all through elementary and high school at the Cathedral Academy in Albany, New York, and had lived on the same block for some of those years. I admired her for being so pretty and nice. Our paths crossed again many years later when coincidentally, her daughter, Rose Rocco, married my brother Dick, who is much younger than I.

Gloria and I became reacquainted at Dick and Rose's house, where we found we had something very profound in common. Each of us had a son who died while in his twenties, a pain we will both carry forever. Gloria's son was killed when an out-of-control car crashed into his car in 1972. She told me how her faith had been her strength and her devotion to Our Lady her consolation.

Feeling she could trust me, Gloria related an experience she had had a year or so after her son had died. She was praying in church, expressing her belief that her son was in heaven, when suddenly she was surrounded by a light. This wasn't an ordinary light, but had a brightness that was indescribable. It became wider and brighter, so much so that she could no longer see the stained glass windows. She felt that she was outdoors, in an expansive, brilliant place. Suddenly she was drenched in peace and a sense of joy so powerful that, to this day, she can hardly talk about it. For Gloria, it was assurance from God that her son was with him.

Gloria asked me not to think of her as a flake. She repeated that this was not her imagination; it really had happened. She didn't have to worry. I believed her. Her experience was rare, grace from God. I saw clearly that this was a beautiful gift given to her by a God who truly remains faithful to us.

Another story convinced me yet again that a faithful God always tries to get our attention. I was the editor of a Connecticut newspaper when Tony Wainwright came to my office one day. He gave me a book which he had published himself after having no luck with established publishers. He told me that he wrote this book after he had faced a series of personal problems which included the death of a daughter, illness, and the loss of a job. He found he had become stronger from his adversities, and he began to wonder if other people had had a similar response from facing traumatic moments.

Wainwright was a journalist when he began writing his book in 1965. He boldly sent letters to almost a thousand well-known people asking if they would write to him and tell him how they had handled a dark moment in their lives. Most never responded, but some who did, like Thomas Merton, were powerful and eloquent.

Tony Wainwright then told me that he had stored the response letters in a cardboard box, waiting almost twenty-five years until finally putting them into a book! Now, I was privileged to get one of the rare copies he had published.

When I read the book, I was most taken by the letter of James C. Penney, founder of the J.C. Penney Company. Penney had sent Tony a piece he had written earlier, titled, "Faith Gave me a New Start at 56." His story began back in 1931, after the stock market crash of 1929 which left him beaten and broke, without an apparent future. Penney found himself a nervous, broken wreck, in a sanitarium, contemplating suicide one terrible night. He wrote:

Somehow that dreadful night passed. The next morning as I shuffled from my room, I heard the sound of singing coming from the mezzanine. The song was a hymn. I will never forget the title. It was *God Will Take Care of You.* I was drawn to the source of that song. A group of patients were holding a prayer meeting. Wearily I joined them. I prayed for God to take care of me, and an amazing thing happened. Suddenly I knew that he would. A profound sense of inner release came over me. The heavy weight seemed lifted from my spirit. That moment marked a turning point in my life.....Maybe at long last I was learning how to pray, by truly submitting myself to the will of God.

What a marvelous moment that must have been for Penney, who learned how faithful God is to us. God gives us the message we need, the one that can get us back into the light, at the moment we are most in the dark. In his testimony he wrote something that is as valid today as back then:

I hadn't realized what had taken place in me. As I rose in wealth and power, dealing in millions of dollars and guiding the activities of thousands of men, I had grown to depend entirely upon my own judgment. My spiritual life had been stored away in a separate compartment. God had very little hand in my everyday thinking.

Yet God had remained faithful to him. Life changed remarkably for Penney after that morning. He went back to work for his own company, but with a modest salary. He completely sized down his lifestyle and began the long climb back. And from then on, he carried a piece of paper with him which gave him strength. On it were the words of the ninety-first Psalm: "He shall cover thee with his feathers, and under his wings shalt thou trust. His truth shall be thy shield and buckler."

Penney was forever grateful that he had gained what was most important: spiritual wealth. He wrote, "I had finally turned to God for guidance in all the acts and decisions of my life."

Another letter received by Wainwright was written by Senator Everett McKinley Dirksen, a man who was well-known in his time as "a legend in the Senate, a legend in Illinois." The Senator related what had happened to him back in 1948, when he developed chorio-retinitis, a condition seriously affecting both eyes. Doctors wanted to remove one eye. The Senator was on his way to the hospital to see about having the operation when he decided to pray for guidance. When he got to the hospital, he told the doctors that he would not have the operation. Dirksen wrote:

> The surgeon found it a bit difficult to understand when I told him that I summoned the aid of another doctor who advised me not to part with an eye and when I told him that it was a much bigger Doctor who lived away upstairs in the sky, the surgeon found it a bit difficult to understand. In fact, he thought it was incredible....This eye has caused me no trouble down through the years.

A miracle? Maybe. Certainly this was an incredible story of faith, one that expressed utter trust in God, the "Doctor" Senator Dirksen called on for help.

The common good

There is yet another important dimension of faith being emphasized more and more by our nation's bishops, and that is our civic and political responsibility to work for the common good. In late 1999 the United States Catholic Bishops issued a document titled *Faithful Citizenship: Civic Responsibility for a New Millennium.* They wrote,

This is a time to bring together the guidance of the Gospel and the opportunities of our democracy to shape a society more respectful of human life and dignity and more committed to justice and peace.

Building peace, combating poverty and despair, and protecting freedom and human rights are not only moral imperatives; they are wise national priorities.

The call to faithful citizenship raises a fundamental question. What does it mean to be a believer and a citizen in the year 2000 and beyond? As Catholics, we can celebrate the Jubilee by recommitting ourselves to carry the values of the Gospel and church teaching into the public square....This dual calling of faith and citizenship is at the heart of what it means to be a Catholic in the United States as we look with hope to the beginning of a new millennium.

A year earlier, the U.S. Catholic Bishops had issued a document called *Everyday Christianity: To Hunger and Thirst for Justice*, which spelled out what it means to be a person of faith in the world.

Catholicism does not call us to abandon the world, but to help shape it. This does not mean leaving worldly tasks and responsibilities, but transforming them....Our entire community of faith must help Catholics be instruments of God's grace and creative power in business and politics, factories and offices, in homes and schools and in all the events of daily life. The vocation to pursue justice is not simply an individual task...it is a call to work with others to humanize and shape the institutions that touch so many people.

The church's social mission is advanced by teachers and scientists, by family farmers and bankers, by salespersons and entertainers. The Catholic social mission is also carried forward by believers who join unions, neighborhood organizations, business groups, civic associations [and the like]. The social mission of the church belongs to all of us. It is an essential part of what it is to be a believer.

The way I see it, there are three responses to the faith challenge put forth by our bishops—to stay put, to stay safe, or not to stay at all. To stay put means to remain immature and in no danger of growing. I call this "love of chair" because this response reminds me of a weekly segment on a TV show my children used to watch when they were tots. The segment was like a brief soap opera, and it was called "Love of Chair." Each week a new episode showed the main and only character, a young man, stuck to his chair. He loved his chair so much that he wouldn't leave it. This meant he couldn't leave his room or his house. He heard the activity of the world outside his window, but every time he got tempted to look out or get involved, he would panic, realizing this meant he would have to leave his chair. And so he would rush back to the safety of his chair, hanging on for dear life.

We are like that sometimes. We hang on to our own safety and security. We won't give up our chair to do the other-focused work Christ asks because we are scared stiff of risking the pain of growth and movement. The result is we give up on love and life and faith. Christians cannot love the chair, cannot stay put.

To stay safe means to make excuses for not growing. People who are afraid of disrupting their comfort can find fifty ways to avoid an opportunity to love. We all know these people. They feel they are not good enough to teach in the religious education program, join the St. Vincent de Paul Society, support low-income housing, raise money for earthquake victims, and so forth. They are full of pseudo-humble excuses: they are not smart enough, strong enough, good enough, no free time, whatever.

People who play it safe are caught in exactly the same syndrome as those who are "looking out for number one." These ways of acting are two sides of the same coin, self-interest, and they block our ability to love others. Christians cannot be focused only on self.

The third response to the faith challenge is not to stay at all but to move, to make a choice and commitment to be human and whole, loving "one another as I [Christ] have loved you." This commitment means we choose a lifestyle that reflects the authentic model and blueprint of Christ, not the current lifestyles and self-serving trends.

Christians must choose the third response or we are taking the name "Christian" in vain. We have the ability and the power to make this choice because we have been given the gift of baptism, which brought us into the community of faith. Baptized in Christ's church, we are the special, chosen ones because we are privy to the truthful call, the call to enter into a growing relationship of love with God, which will make us human, whole, and mature.

This is the ultimate call issued by the Master Drummer, who not only sounds the notes but has also provided us with the score. Faith is not silent. It resonates as it is shared in harmony from one to another, becoming an eternal love song.

Each of us has to look at Jesus, listen to him again and again, and allow ourselves to be seduced by what we see and hear. That is the simple, bottom line when we consider what it means to be faith-full. We must believe so much in Jesus that we join forces with him, become his clone, and never back down on our commitment to continue the work he began to make this world the beautiful, just place his Father wants.

Epilogue

When it comes to prayer, there is a gut level question to ask: what is it that we should be praying for if we truly are people of faith, in a loving relationship with God? Shouldn't it be that the two of us—ourselves and our Lover—will always be there for each other, in all kinds of situations? Can we believe that even when we can't feel God responding, that he is? This is where faith comes in, when the big screen is blank and we feel not just abandoned but brutalized by life, forgotten by the God who is supposed to be always good. Maybe in times like this we just aren't looking for God in the right places.

I remember years ago when I was tormented and sick, pregnant for the sixth time and in a failing marriage. God seemed far away and I prayed, not to have this cross end but to show me that he understood the horror of my dark place and still loved me. Unexpectedly, a neighbor came by. She sensed I was sick and brought me some soup. When she saw how distressed I was, she didn't try to give me a pep talk or resort to pious platitudes. She simply put her arm around me and cried with me. That is when I knew God had answered my prayer. In the person of my neighbor, God had shown me his love and assured me I would make it out of the darkness.

We may have a problem trusting that God is with us even when life has beaten us down. This stems back to old ways of describing God, when great emphasis was placed on the power of God. As a child, I remember having a lot of problems with this God who made me afraid. I loved his son Jesus, though, and this made me even madder at God. How could he have loved his son and still send him into the world to die so we could be saved? If he was such a powerful God, couldn't he have saved us without making his son go through that horrible death on the cross?

In my childlike way, I came up with another scenario. I began to believe that Jesus got in big trouble in his homeland because he went around saying things which upset almost everybody. I imagined his mother Mary telling him to be careful, that there were a lot of bad people around and he could get into trouble. When he did make powerful enemies and was killed on the cross, I fantasized that his Father in heaven must have been devastated. But God didn't come down and save Jesus from death; he chose to do something much better. God chose to bring his son back to life and to give this gift of life forever to everybody who loved his son. Now he wasn't a terrible God, in my mind. He was a wonderful, loving God who fixed everything in a way no one could have imagined.

I was a big fan of fairy tales, and I may have gotten this idea about God from *Sleeping Beauty*. In this story, the baby princess receives a curse from one of her jealous fairy godmothers: on her sixteenth birthday, the princess would find a spinning wheel, prick her finger, and die. At the moment the curse is spoken, a good fairy godmother enters. She is devastated by this evil but cannot take the curse away. She can fix it, however, and does so by saying that the princess will not die but sleep for one hundred years, to be awakened then by the loving kiss of a prince.

And so I simply adapted the Sleeping Beauty story to explain God to myself, and this changed all my reservations which had been surfacing about him. God was a lover who transformed death into sleep and promised to awaken each of us with his kiss, just as he had done for his son. Admittedly, this was not theology, but a story that worked for me as a child. Now, in my mature years, I count this imagination as one of the great blessings in my life. It has helped me learn to trust God, believing that he would always know how to "fix" what goes wrong in our lives.

Even when my faith was strained and I felt far away from God, I know now that the trust I had learned as a child was always there. How many times I prayed for my son Peter, that he would get well. Sometimes I begged. I silently screamed. But the deeper prayer that came from the core of me was a plea that the Lord help me accept this cross and discover eventually what I was to learn from my son's pain.

When Peter died, I was astounded that pain could be so severe. But even more astounding was that I was given a glimpse of God's mysteries which I never would have been able to comprehend before. Now I know how real God's kiss is; now I know that there is no death, only transformation. In a note he left me before he died, Peter wrote that he was "going home." Now my faith, my growing relationship with God, embraces the two "homes" of earth and heaven in a way I could not have imagined. My faith has taken on what I can only call a cosmic dimension.

I still fall into the trap of sometimes offering narrow and limited prayers, telling God what I want instead of asking what he wants for me. In this regard, Louis Evely gave us something to think about when he wrote, "God won't appear to us on our level. We'll understand him only if we speak his language." And where do we learn God's language? In "God's book," says Evely, the Bible. When we read a passage, "we must think of it, not as a text to be perused or an idea to be dissected, but as God himself coming into our tent to speak to us face to face as a person speaks to a friend." That is how a relationship works, isn't it?

If we have problems accepting God's ways, it may be simply because we are just human. As weak human beings, we all want the good life, the easy life, the comfortable life, the successful life. And so we pray for those things that make us feel good. But most of us learn that life has something else in store for us, a rocky road scattered with thistles and thorns.

I have come to learn there is a wisdom in this scenario. It has something to do with making us into beautiful people who are compassionate, loving, non-judgmental, gentle. As someone put it, "The heart that breaks is the heart that can contain the world." If life is too comfortable, too safe, who needs God? I think faith has much to do with welcoming the blows and setbacks that make us look and act more like the One we are related to.

I remember a story told by a priest, in answer to a woman whose faith was being shaken by the difficulties of her life. He told her that in Latin America, one of the industries was making rugs by hand. The people making the rugs would sit under the looms as they worked the colored yarn. From where they sat they could see only a crisscross of patterns, which seemed to make no sense, and feel the discomfort of the knots. Yet for anyone standing who could see the top side of the rug, the view was different, for they could see the finished product, the beautiful pattern that had been woven by the worker.

The priest said that life is like being on the underside of the rug. There we see only the mish-mash of threads and feel the bumps from the knots. But, oh, on the other side, something beautiful is happening. And the more confusion of color and the more knots, the more elegant the result. When we leave this earth, it is then that God will show us the beautiful pattern we have been weaving all the while, and we will understand his ways.

When I reflect on some of the faith-full people I have met in my lifetime, I get a sneak preview of the beautiful pattern God is designing while I am still on the underside of my existence, limited in my vision. In all my experiences, in all my pain, in all my prayers, I have come to know it is faith—my relationship with the Triune God—that has given me the light to continually see life as a great adventure with a great future. Now I can be simple enough to use fairy-tale language about my God, knowing that no prick of the spinning wheel will ever kill me because my Lover has kissed me. And so there is no permanent death—only permanent life.

Thomas Merton memorably expressed the meaning of faith in a thought worth pondering. He wrote,

> But above all, faith is the opening of an inward eye, the eye of the heart, to be filled with the presence of Divine light. Ultimately faith is the only key to the universe. The final meaning of human existence, and the answers to questions on which all our happiness depends cannot be reached in any other way.

To that I say, "Amen!"

Resources

Barrett, Michael. *The Silent Stream*. Plainfield, CT: Serenity Press, 2000.

Barron, Robert E. *And Now I See: A Theology of Transformation*. New York: Crossroad Publishing, 1998.

Berman, Philip L., ed. *The Courage to Grow Old*. New York: Ballantine Books, 1989.

Blake, William. *Selection of Poems and Letters*, Penguin Books, 1958.

Bruteau, Beatrice. *The Easter Mysteries*. New York: Crossroad Publishing, 1995.

Bucke, Richard Maurice. *Cosmic Consciousness: A Study in the Evolution of the Human Mind*. New York: Carol Publishing Group, 1993.

Cepress, Celestine, ed. *Sister Thea Bowman: Shooting Star*. Winona, MN: St. Mary's Press, 1993.

Chesterton, G.K. *The Everlasting Man*. San Francisco: Ignatius Press, 1993.

D'Arcy, Paula. *The Gift of the Red Bird*. New York: Crossroad Publishing, 1996.

D'Souza, Dinesh. *The Catholic Classics*, Vol. 1 (1986) & Vol. 2 (1989). Huntington, IN: Our Sunday Visitor Publishing.

Davis, Rebecca and Susan Mesner, eds. *The Treasury of Religious and Spiritual Quotations*. Pleasantville, NY: Reader's Digest, 1994.

de Chardin, Pierre Teilhard. *How I Believe*. New York: Harper & Row, 1969.

Douglas, James W. *The Non-Violent Coming of God*. Maryknoll, NY: Orbis Books, 1991.

Emerson, Ralph Waldo. *Emerson's Essays*. New York: HarperTrade, 1981.

Evely, Louis. *In His Presence*. New York: Image Books (Doubleday), 1974.

Evely, Louis. *That Man Is You*. Mahwah, NJ: Paulist Press, 1964.

Gushurst, Frederick, ed. *The Quotable Fulton Sheen*. Anderson, SC: Droke House, 1967.

Holloway, Richard. *Anger, Sex, Doubt and Death*. London: SPCK, 1992.

Howden, F. Newton. *Life Here and Hereafter*. Sewanee, TN: Proctor's Hall Press (Cascade Pubs.), 1992.

James, William. *The Varieties of Religious Experience*. New York: Collier Books, 1961.

Küng, Hans. *Eternal Life? Life after Death as a Medical, Philosophical, and Theological Problem.* New York: Crossroad Publishing, 1991.

Lewis, C.S. *A Grief Observed.* New York: HarperCollins, 1994.

Lewis, C.S. *Mere Christianity.* New York: S & S Trade, 1997.

Liebman, Joshua Loth. *Peace of Mind.* New York: Simon and Schuster, 1946.

Martin, James, ed. *How Can I Find God? The Famous and Not-So-Famous Consider the Quintessential Question.* Ligouri, MO: Triumph Books, 1997.

Merton, Thomas. *New Seeds of Contemplation.* New York: New Directions Press.

Morris, Debbie. *Forgiving the Dead Man Walking: Only One Woman Can Tell the Entire Story.* New York: HarperCollins, 1998.

Murrow, Edward R. *This I Believe.* Simon and Schuster, 1954.

Price, Eugenia. *No Pat Answers.* Grand Rapids, MI: Zondervan, 1983.

Somerville, James M. *The Mystical Sense of the Gospels: A Handbook for Contemplatives.* New York: Crossroad Publishing, 1997.

Thomas, Lewis. *The Lives of a Cell: Notes of a Biology Watcher.* New York: Viking Penguin, 1978.

United States Catholic Bishops. *Everyday Christianity: To Hunger and Thirst for Justice.* Washington, DC: USCC Publishing.

Vann, Gerald. *The Seven Sweet Blessings of Christ: And How to Make Them Yours* (original title: *The Divine Pity*). Manchester, NH: Sophia Institute Press, 1997.

Wainwright, Anthony. *Moment of Truth.* Miami, FL: KAR Printing, Inc., 1990.

Walley, Dean, ed. *All Men Seek God.* Kansas City, MO: Hallmark Editions, 1968.

Whitman, Walt. *Complete Poetry and Selected Prose.* Miller, J.E., ed. Boston: Houghton Mifflin, 1972.

Wilkes, Paul. *Beyond the Walls: Monastic Wisdom for Everyday Life.* New York: Doubleday, 1999.

Wink, Walter. *Engaging the Powers: Discernment and Resistance in a World of Domination.* Minneapolis, MN: Augsburg Fortress, 1992.

Wordsworth, William. *Selected Poetry.* Van Doren, Mark, ed. New York: Modern Library (Random House), 1950.

—. *God's Treasury of Virtues.* Edited by Honor Books staff. Tulsa, OK: Honor Books, 1996.

Of Related Interest...

Coincidences
Touched by a Miracle
Antoinette Bosco

Collected here is a kaleidoscope of stories about real people from all walks of life who experienced what might be called a "remarkable coincidence" in their lives. Are the patterns of their life stories really random? Or is there an underlying design that reveals the hand and presence of Someone who cares?   0-89622-749-9, 208 pp, $12.95 (B-81)

The Pummeled Heart
Finding Peace Through Pain
Antoinette Bosco

This touching and amazing story of one woman's struggle to confront many forms of suffering offers a model of how trust and hope in God gives strength to overcome evil. Readers will want to share this book with others.
0-89622-584-4, 140 pp, $9.95 (W-45)

Healing Wounded Emotions
Overcoming Life's Hurts
Martin Padovani

A best-seller for over a decade, this book explains how our emotional and spiritual lives interact. Challenges readers to live fuller, more satisfying lives.
0-89622-333-7, 128 pp, $7.95 (W-22)

Everyday Epiphanies
Seeing the Sacred in Every Thing
Melannie Svoboda, SND

Offers 175 short stories, divided according to the seasons of the year and ending with a reflection prayer. Topics range from setting the table, getting the mail, rain, putting away groceries, and working, to the uncommon occasions that we all look forward to and relish when they occur.
0-89622-730-8, 192 pp, $9.95 (B-45)

Available at religious bookstores or from:

TWENTY-THIRD PUBLICATIONS
PO BOX 180 · 185 WILLOW STREET ⬩ MYSTIC, CT 06355 · 1-800-321-0411
FAX: 1-800-572-0788 BAYARD E-MAIL: ttpubs@aol.com

Call for a free catalog